## Donated
## To The Library by

MARYKNOLL COMMUNITY, NY

# THE BUDDHIST
# CONCEPT OF HELL

# THE BUDDHIST
# CONCEPT OF HELL

by

DAIGAN and ALICIA MATSUNAGA

PHILOSOPHICAL LIBRARY
New York

The six full page illustrations appearing in this book are #1-6 "From Hell Screen," property of Tokyo National Museum, reprinted from *Nippon Emakimono Zenshū* by the courtesy of Kadokawa Shoten.

# TABLE OF CONTENTS

Introduction .................................................................................... vii

## SECTION ONE

## HISTORICAL DEVELOPMENT AND PHILOSOPHICAL SIGNIFICANCE OF THE CONCEPT OF HELL

CHAPTER

I. BACKGROUND — VEDIC ORIGIN OF HELL ........     13

II. THE SIGNIFICANCE OF HELL IN EARLY BUD-
    DHISM ................................................................     21

    A. The Two Levels of Teaching ...................     23

    B. Naraka and the Principal Doctrines of Early Bud-
       dhism .........................................................     28

    C. Early Buddhist Cosmology and Descriptions of
       Naraka ........................................................     39

    D. Hell in Abhidharma Buddhism ...............     43

III. HELL IN MĀHĀYANA BUDDHISM ..............     47

    A. Nāgārjuna and the Mādhyamika View of Human
       Existence .....................................................     49

    B. Concept of Emptiness ...........................     54

    C. The Concept of Hell in Vijñānavāda Philosophy ....     60

## SECTION TWO

## ANALYSIS AND INTERPRETATION OF THE EIGHT BUDDHIST HELLS PRESENTED BY THE SUTRA OF THE REMEMBRANCE OF THE TRUE LAW

IV. DESCRIPTION AND ANALYSIS OF THE EIGHT
HELLS .................................................................... 75
    A. The Text ............................................ 75
    B. Background and Setting ............................. 76
    C. Significance of the Hells ........................... 78
    D. Contents of the Eight Buddhist Hells .............. 80
        1. Saṃjīva (Hell of Repetition) ................ 81
        2. Kāla-sūtra (Black-rope Hell) ................ 85
        3. Saṃghāta (Crowded Hell) ................... 87
        4. Raurava (Screaming Hell) ................... 90
        5. Mahāraurava (Great Screaming Hell) ......... 92
        6. Tapana (Hell of Burning Heat) ............. 94
        7. Pratapana (Hell of Great Burning Heat) ...... 97
        8. Avīci (No-Interval Hell) ................... 99
    Appendix ............................................. 107
    Footnotes ............................................ 137
    Bibliography ......................................... 145
    Index ................................................ 149

# INTRODUCTION

Buddhism inherited a long tradition from India, its mother country, that it never chose to completely discard despite its various journeys; beneath the native garb of the countries it chose to make its home, the Indian features always remained apparent. The concept of hell was one such Indian characteristic that accompanied Buddhism into every nation that it entered. Perhaps this grim attendant was never set aside because its universal nature touched upon a dim archetype dwelling within each individual. For just as every child experiences fear of the dark, so the grown up child is secretly frightened by the darkness he knows exists within himself. The naive and unsophisticated have always been capable of projecting this fear exteriorly into a tangible place they call hell while their more worldly counterparts in contemporary society seek rational explanations through modern techniques of probing the mind. For the Buddhist Enlightened One, hell can neither be projected outwards nor be explored by the hands of another within — it is the result of one's own creation that can only be discovered and cleansed away by means of self-reflection.

"Hell" has become one of the most emotionally charged words in the human language and the moment it is mentioned an immediate stereotype comes to mind. For most contemporaries, hell is an outdated device created to frighten the ignorant masses into social or religious conformity. It is also a term that is inseparably linked with fear and even the modern man who denounces the concept as superstition still responds interiorly to the spell of the word as a reminder of the mysterious unknown. Death, man's greatest unknown has provided one of the main sources of nourishment for the concept of hell.

There is no question that hell has been used as a device of fear by all major religions and Buddhism is no exception. For Buddhists it represented one of the most practical methods of teaching naive and unsophisticated individuals the need to practice virtue. Just as children are taught by using simple concrete explanations, so at the conventional level, the symbolism of hell was taught as the first step on the path towards religious awareness. To explain to a child that the demons of the hells will punish him if he lies by pulling out his tongue may induce fear but is not nearly as fearful or confusing as to tell him that if he lies he will create his own hell in which symbolically he will tear out his own tongue. Superficially such teachings appear to be deceptions, but then in the Buddhist view all human speech is a form of deception and it is merely a matter of degree. Attempting to explain the meaning of Enlightenment by means of dichotomic human speech becomes only slightly less deceptive than teaching a child the existence of hell as a place of punishment. Unfortunately few individuals in modern society update their religious study beyond childhood and as a result they either cling to or reject the simple tangible explanations directed to the mind of a child. This has happened in Buddhism just as in the other great religions. A great chasm has come to exist between the learned theologians and priests and the not-so learned laity and countryside clergy. Faith and knowledge have taken separate paths and modern intellectuals quickly point to the path of faith as proof of the degeneracy of the religion. In this struggle, the concept of hell is one of the first beliefs to be attacked as an illogical and unscientific teaching utilized as an instrument of fear. Buddhist theologians on the other hand, tend to dwell aloof, concerned with minute textual comparisons and apparently oblivious of the need to bridge the spiritual chasm and share their knowledge with the no longer unsophisticated and naive laity.

During the time of the historical Buddha and for many centuries thereafter, the masses were incapable of intellectually understanding the more profound philosophy taught to the clergy. This situation still exists in certain underdeveloped countries where the rate of literacy is low but in modern nations like Japan, the situation has drastically changed and Buddhism has failed to keep pace. Its teachings are still geared to the level of the unsophisticated countryside populace and although it is possible for many individuals to intuitively realise a profound meaning by following the path of faith,[1] the modern urban dweller lacks the patience to bother with such seemingly naive views. This is the problem in approaching an understanding of the real significance of the Buddhist concept of hell. For centuries two views of the concept have existed side by side. The first was the tangible symbolism of a place of suffering and retribution presented to the laity in order to encourage the practice of virtue; while the second was a more profound view held by the clergy and theologians who no longer needed tangible symbols on the path to spiritual awareness. The first view, because of its potent dramatic and universal nature, gained predominance while the second was relegated to learned writings and meditation halls. Very rarely in modern times has anyone mentioned the fact that a second view even existed in Buddhism, let alone that such a view has a centuries old tradition.[2]

The aim of this work is to present a philosophical explanation of the Buddhist concept of hell that explores its more profound meaning and theoretical foundation. The view will be primarily "Mahāyāna" since it is based upon Mādhyamika and Vijñānavāda thought and the first section of this work deals with the historical development of the concept. The second section presents a description of the actual Buddhist hells that is drawn from a "Hīnayāna" text entitled the *Sutra of the Remembrance of the True Law* (*Saddharma-smṛti-upasthāna*) with an analysis of the moral significance of each Buddhist hell. Although the sutra used is officially classified in the Chinese canon as a "Hīnayāna" text, its descriptions complement the Mahāyāna philosophical conception of hell and offer vivid symbolism of man's struggle to eliminate the dark shadows dwelling within himself.

SECTION ONE

# HISTORICAL DEVELOPMENT AND PHILOSOPHICAL SIGNIFICANCE OF THE CONCEPT OF HELL

# CHAPTER I

# BACKGROUND – VEDIC ORIGIN OF HELL

The oldest Indian allusions to what can be defined as hell date back to the *Ṛg Veda*, although scholars have long debated the significance of these early appearances.[1] Here the Vedic poets voiced their fears of the dark pit or stygian abyss that has universally haunted man. They pleaded that the wicked might be cast down and destroyed, yet sought protection for themselves against such a fate:

Indra and Soma, plunge the wicked in the
　depth, yea, cast them into darkness that hath no support.

So that not one of them may ever thence return
　so may your wrathful might prevail and conquer them.

RV VII. 104,3[2]

Turn yourselves hitherward this day, ye Holy,
　that fearing in my heart I may approach you.
Protect us, God; let not the wolf destroy us,
　save us, ye Holy, from the pit and falling.

RV II. 29,6[3]

They visualized this as the land of chaos, of no-return; the realm of destruction and despair. It is no wonder they did not seek to dwell upon it and preferred to turn their aspirations to the heavens. Looking above, they could gaze in wonder at the majestic order of the stars and feel, just as generations following them were to believe, that man's hope issued forth from the brightness and purity of the heavenly universe.

Although in the *Ṛg Veda* there is little discussion regarding the nature of death or fate of the deceased, we do learn that ordinary mortals had little danger of falling into the pit, which was the place of demons, sorcerers and conspirators.[4] The main abode of the dead was the shining heaven of the Fathers (*Pitṛ*), who dwelt with their King Yama, the First Ancestor. Here the poets could aspire to be born:

> The kingdom of inexhaustible light,
> Whence is derived the radiance of the sun,
> To this kingdom transport me,
> Eternal, undying.
>
> RV IX. 113,7[5]

The only fear common men faced was the possibility of straying from the path on their way to this heaven and being devoured by demons. In order to avoid such a peril, the watch-dogs of Yama were invoked to serve as guardians and protectors:

> And those two dogs of thine, Yama, the watchers,
>     four eyed, who look on men and guard the pathway
> Entrust this man, O King, to their protection, and
>     with prosperity and health endow him.
> Dark-hued, insatiate, with distended nostrils, Yama's
>     two envoys roam among the people;
> May they restore to us a fair existence here and to-day,
>     that we may see the sunlight.
>
> RV X. 14, 11-12[6]

There is no mention whether these dogs bestowed their protection on all or merely the just. In fact, there is no mention of the fate of simple erring mortals or any clear concept of judgment. The land of the Fathers appeared to be a mere extenuation of the present life. There were rewards however, for the pious based

14

upon the merits they had accumulated during their earthly
sojourn:

> Go forth, go forth upon those ancient pathways
> by which our former fathers have departed.
> Thou shalt behold god Varuṇa and Yama,
> both Kings, in funeral offerings rejoicing.

> Unite thou with the Fathers and with Yama,
> with *iṣṭāpūrta* in the highest heaven.
> Leaving behind all blemish homeward hie thee
> and all-resplendent join thee with a body.

RV X. 14,7-8[7]

Here *iṣṭāpūrta* refers to sacrificial merits (*iṣṭa*) and good works
(*pūrta*) which would be awaiting the deceased upon his arrival
in heaven.[8] This was a germ of the later concept of karma that
so greatly influenced Indian morality.[9]

Although the *Ṛg Veda* presents a complex liturgy, the world
view remained quite primitive in that man had not yet encountered
a form of suffering to shake him to the depths of his existential
being. He felt intimately united with the universe surrounding
him and did not yet perceive a fearful chasm between life and
death since he had not yet turned to self-reflection and developed
a conscious awareness of his own individuality. The after-world
was a continuation of the present life where man could enjoy
the same pleasures as he had on earth without the disadvantages
of human imperfections.[10] In time, as self-consciousness gradually
came to life, the attitude towards death began to change. Becoming aware of his own ego, man sought to preserve and
extend his self-identity. He was no longer content to fade into the
anonymous world of the dead but began to place importance
upon the here and now. Such self-reflection with its ensuing
evaluation of human existence lead to an increased fear of death.
We can find this new attitude clearly expressed in the *Atharva
Veda* where references to death are much more abundant:

> 7. Thy mind shall not go thither, shall not disappear!

Do not become heedless of the living, do not follow the
Fathers!
All the gods shall preserve thee here!
8. Do not long after the departed, who conduct (men) afar!
Ascend from the darkness, come to the light! We lay hold
of thy hands.
9. The two dogs of Yama, the black and the brindled one,
that guard the road (to heaven), that have been despatched,
shall not (go after) thee! Come hither, do not long to be
away; do not tarry here with thy mind turned to a
distance!
10. Do not follow this path: it is terrible! I speak of that by
which thou has not hitherto gone. Darkness is this, O man,
do not enter it! Danger is beyond, security here for thee.

VIII I. 7-10[11]

The moment man became aware of the meaning of human life,
he began to cling to living and regard death as a fearful uncer-
tainty. No doubt in the earlier period some sensitive individuals
must have experienced such fears but now it becomes a massed
cry. Painfully it had become evident that the promised joys
of Yama's heaven could not be attained without leaving the
safety of the present world behind. But despite the increased
awareness of death in the *Atharva Veda,* this period still did not
present any clear notion of a path to hell, judgment, or transmigration. Such were left to later eras where an even greater self-
consciousness began to search for the means to attain immortality.
The beginning of the concept of retribution appears in the
*Śatapatha Brāhmaṇa* where the famous statement is found, "For
whatever food, a man eats in this world, by the very same
is he eaten again"[12] and elsewhere, "a man is born into the
world that he has made."[13] Such a movement further demonstrates the growth of human awareness. If all the deceased are
allowed to enter the heaven of the Fathers, then what is the
reward for virtue and punishment for evil? Observing that
justice does not necessarily triumph in the present life, man can
only imagine that eventually the good must be rewarded and

the wicked punished in the next life. Although there is not a clear view of what the hereafter is like in the *Brāhmaṇas*, the desire for justice has taken root. We can also note that a distinction is now made between the path of the Fathers and the way to the deva heavens[14] with special sacrifices being deemed efficacious in reaching the domains of certain gods.[15] Man's desire to attain immortality has now become apparent but this desire is still confined to a type of individual immortality that is finally developed into a doctrine of transmigration in the *Upaniṣads,* the time of supreme self-awareness.

Once vision is turned inwards, the flaws of human nature become strikingly apparent. The body is frail, subject to sickness and death while the will is weak and unsteady. Self-reflection will ultimately drive anyone to seek for a higher goal than the fulfillment of ordinary desires:

> O Maghavan, verily, this body (*śarīra*) is mortal. It has been appropriated by Death (*mṛtyu*). [But] it is the standing-ground of that deathless, bodiless Self (*Ātman*). Verily, he who is incorporate has been appropriated by pleasure and pain. Verily, there is no freedom from pleasure and pain for one while he is incorporate. Verily, while one is bodiless, pleasure and pain do not touch him.
>
> Chāndogya Upaniṣad VIII. 12,1[16]

The search within leads to the desire for a permanent lasting Self. A Self freed from suffering, pain and torment that will never die and never betray man's faith. And in his search for perfection, man molds the entire universe to suit his own glorified image and finds therein his ultimate perfection. For although the individual may be weak and finite, the universe presents him with the feeling of eternal order and perfection. He is awed by its magnitude and lasting endurance. It relentlessly repeats its constant cycle of seasons while man and all other finite objects wither and die after merely a few short summers. This indeed would be a Self worthy of trust. But the question of justice still remains. If man is to trust something beyond himself, then he must also believe that born out of his trust, he will find justice in his dealings with his fellow men. It is not right that the wicked should seem to prosper and attain heaven while the good must undergo adversity. The acute awareness of his sense of justice forces him to separate those who choose to follow base instincts from those who seek higher goals. Thus the view develops that as man acts, he creates his own future, which represents the product of his actions. If that future is not to be fulfilled in this world, then it must take place in the hereafter. The influence of actions alone must survive after the dissolution of man and relentlessly go on to determine the future. Such a realization is clear in the famous dialogue between Yajñavalkya and Jāralkārava Ārtabhāga:

> . . . 'When a man dies, what does not leave him?'
> 'The name. Endless, verily, is the name. Endless are the All-gods. An endless world he wins thereby.'
> . . . 'When the voice of a dead man goes into fire, his breath into wind, his eye into the sun, his mind into the moon, his hearing into the quarters of heaven, his body into the earth, his soul (*ātman*) into space, the hairs of his head into plants, the hairs of his body into trees, and his blood and semen are placed in water, what then becomes of his person (*puruṣa*)?'
> . . . The two went away and deliberated, what they said was *karma* (action). What they praised was *karma*. Verily, one becomes good by good action, bad by bad action.
> Bṛhadāraṇyaka Upaniṣad III. 2, 12,13[17]

Actions become the basis of morality, the influences that survive the physical destruction of man and determine the future:

> Accordingly, those who are of pleasant conduct here — the prospect is, indeed, that they will enter a pleasant womb, either the womb of a Brahman, or the womb of a Kshatriya, or the womb of a Vaishya. But those who are of stinking conduct here — the prospect is, indeed, that they will enter a stinking womb, either the womb of a dog, or the womb of a swine, or the womb of an outcast (*caṇḍāla*).
> Chāndogya Upaniṣad V. 10.7[18]

Such a theory creates a potent moral law for the masses. It is no wonder that the concept of reincarnation spread popularly throughout India. The philosophers were to raise further questions and some were even to reject the belief in karma entirely,[19] but the masses were satisfied. They had found a way to make justice triumph.

As man began his inner search for transcendent immortality, the deva (heavenly spirits) began to drop in esteem. They were no longer regarded as supreme realities since man had already transcended them and now their heavens appeared as tarnished goals. Gradually these heavens begin their drop into the realm of saṃsāra or 'birth and death.' No longer conceived of as abodes of eternal repose now they are merely places of temporary happiness. But even as such they still remained a satisfactory goal in the minds of large segments of the masses who sought a tangible goal.

The transition away from the belief in the deva heavens as ideal goals was not immediate and the *Upaniṣads* first sought to harmonize with the older beliefs. Three different pathways after death were presented.[20] One path led to the devas (*devayāna*) and was called the path of light (*arcismārga*). At first this was the way to union with the deity Brahmā and ultimately, as such a notion was transcended, to unity with the Ultimate. The second way was the *pitṛyāna*, or path of smoke and darkness (*dhūmamārga*). This road led to a reward for good deeds but it did not go on to further heights. Its followers eventually returned to earth since they still remained within the clutches of saṃsāra. The third pathway led to the realm of darkness and desolation. It was upon this road that creatures who live and die, worms, insects and creeping things went crawling along.[21]

In view of such a transition the glory of the kingdom of Yama began to wane. Although he still remained a great god worthy of reverence and veneration, his kingdom was no longer a goal to be sought. Eventually, with the growing notion of retribution, he became linked with the idea of justice and transformed into the deity who decides the fate of the deceased. By the time of the *Mahābhārata*, when Yama receives the title "Dharmarāja" or King of justice this idea has prevailed and he is viewed as a fearful chastiser of the wicked, often portrayed as having a grim appearance with a dark green complexion and glowing red eyes, dressed in blood red garments.

Thus the cycle is complete — from the vague abstract notions of a land of death representing the continuation of the present life to the rise of human awareness, bringing with it concepts of justice and the belief in a moral order governed by the law of actions (*karma*). Such was the inheritance of Buddhism, upon which new concepts of salvation and hell were to be constructed.

# CHAPTER II

# THE SIGNIFICANCE OF HELL IN EARLY BUDDHISM

During the sixth century B.C. when Buddhism arose in India, the nation was experiencing a social and intellectual ferment. New ideas and philosophies were coming to light just as old kingdoms and social orders began to wane. Philosophers were engaged in the defense or spirited rejection of the Vedas, Brāhmaṇas and early Upaniṣads, while the laity still clung to their beliefs in the great Vedic gods as well as local chthonic spirits and deities. Countless varieties of sorcery, magic and witchcraft abounded.[1] Belief in the doctrine of karma was widespread but it tended to have a strong fatalistic tone and was coupled with the concept of a physical transmigration. Despite this, the belief in karma deeply appealed to the laity since it presented them with a logical explanation for life. Those enduring suffering or hardship could comfort themselves in believing their present fate was the result of past actions and that if they patiently endured it while continuing to lead a moral life, they would be assured of a pleasant state in the next life. Such a literal understanding of transmigration also led individuals to obtain a certain appreciation of the interrelated nature of all existents, for if someone believed that in a past life he might have been an animal or insect, possessed of various shades of colour; then he would feel a closer living relationship with all creatures and beings. If he harmed another, it could even be tantamount to injuring a former parent or loved one. Such a belief tended to create a spontaneous attitude of love and compassion towards all that eventually developed into the doctrine of *ahiṃsā* (nonviolence).[2] But these popular beliefs also generated a great number of moral flaws, the most outstanding of which was a form of moral turpitude.

During his lifetime, the historical Buddha strongly attacked the belief in fatalistic karma and the reliance upon deities since such attitudes encouraged individuals to evade their present responsibility to lead a moral life.[3] They encouraged passivism and even extremes of escapism that thwarted true spiritual progress. After all, if one's life was already predetermined, why bother to labor or practice virtue? In the same vein, if a deity could be invoked to solve all the human problems, the only concern would be in attempting to please the deity and direct responsibility to oneself for one's own actions could be avoided. The historical Buddha sought to remedy such moral ills by placing the responsibility for the individual's fate directly into his own hands. For the laity this still had to be done with qualifications since they demanded a tangible goal. It was not sufficient to point out to them how improper actions would lead to future suffering unless the forms of suffering or reward could be clearly defined. The layman was not about to practice virtue in hope of some vague reward as long as he could observe his friends presently enjoying the delights of being wicked. He was pragmatic enough to want to have his reward for virtue clearly spelt out for him and the only method by which the Buddhists could do this was to revert to some level of understandable symbolism. How natural it was to thus point to the most deeply imbedded instinctual feelings within man — the love for light and fear of darkness particularly since such experiences had already been translated into the Indian concept of the deva heavens and dark pit of hell. The individual's fate was once again placed into his own hands since his own personal actions determined his symbolic fate. Grasped as a tangible, belief in the heavens and hells was a concrete reality projected into the after-life. On the other hand, the heavens also served as a temporary goal acting as a form of mental preparation. Once the individual was capable of progressing beyond the symbolism into the philosophical meaning, then the ultimate goal of Enlightenment could be attained. This latter was the only goal generally taught to the monks and these diverse presentations represent what was known as the two levels of teaching.

## A. *The Two Levels of Teaching*

In Early Buddhism, or the Buddhism practiced during the lifetime of the historical Buddha and by his disciples shortly after his death, it is generally possible to discern two distinct levels of teaching; the first directed towards the religious community, and the second for the laity engaged in worldly pursuits. These distinctions were not always strictly observed since in some cases, certain monks were not spiritually advanced beyond the laity while many laymen possessed profound knowledge. It was thus essential to present gradations in the teaching in accord with the general understanding of the audiences.

These two forms of teaching did not represent two distinct methods of salvation but rather were two different levels of religious awareness. The teaching directed towards the laity had the initial goal of leading them to reach the monk's level of understanding, whereby they would then be able to comprehend and practice the more abstract philosophical doctrines. In other words, it was a form of preparation based upon the needs of the contemporary society which was relatively unsophisticated in the modern sense.

For the average layman of this period, the belief in the existence of deva heavens inhabited by the great deities of the Vedas was still the order of the day. Depending upon the time and locality, certain deva were considered superior and their heavens deemed to be more desirable abodes. In contrast to the heavens, the contemporary world view accepted the existence of various forms of hell for the wicked. Such beliefs were capable of successfully promoting morality while at the same time gradually developing a religious awareness. It also was the language of the day and if anyone in speaking to the laity departed too far from this idiom, he was apt to be laughed at or thought insane. It would be comparable in modern times to the devotion to science and logic where miracle workers or those who might claim to be able to walk on water or float in the air are considered charlatans. To the people of ancient India, the deva and their heavens were as real as modern beliefs in the powers of wonder drugs and merely represented an early phase of man's eternal search for the fountain of life. The Buddhists utilized such contemporary beliefs as forms of *upāya* or 'skillful means' to instruct the laity along the preliminary steps of the spiritual path. *Upāya* were not merely directed towards the laity since even the teachings for the monks ultimately fell into the realm of skillful means leading the individual on to attain his own understanding of truth (Enlightenment).

The most popular method of instruction for the laity in Early Buddhism was known as the three *kathā* or graduated forms of discourse.[4] These consisted of *dāna kathā* (a discussion on the benefits of offering), followed by *sīla kathā* (discourse on proper discipline or morality), and finally *sagga kathā*, whereby the laity was promised that if they properly practiced offering and morality, they would attain sufficient virtue (*puñña*) to be born into a deva heaven. Conversely, those who failed to practice offerings and morality could anticipate falling into hell. The logic behind these was to promote a basic understanding of the Buddhist law of karma whereby the individual's own good actions would lead to future good results and vice versa. As a natural consequence of such a method of teaching, the layman's goal became the acquisition of *puñña* (merit) in order to attain future reward in a happy heaven. Fundamentally, this simple form of morality was not very different from other contemporary Indian popular beliefs, with the exception that it was set forth under the cloak of Buddhism and the taint of fatalism was removed. The Buddhists believed it essential that the layman begin his spiritual life with an understanding of the importance of the law of karma.

Philosophically, karma (Pa. *kamma*) or human conduct and its influence, was divided into three different categories in Early Buddhism. These consisted of wholesome, unwholesome and neutral varieties. Wholesome conduct (*kusala kamma*) was further divided into two different spheres: the first relating to worldly actions (*sava*), which largely pertained to the laity; and the second, to religious or nonworldly actions (*asava*). It was on the level of wholesome *worldly* actions that *puñña* was considered to be merit. To illustrate:

*Wholesome Karma (kusala kamma)*
Asava — Religious nonworldly goodness (*Brahmacariya*)
Sava — Worldly morality (*puñña*) [5]

Although *puñña* signified a form of good conduct, it was believed to be confined mainly to the sphere of worldly morality since its goal was deemed to be birth in a happy heaven. Such a goal in contrast to the Nirvana sought by the monks was considered worldly, and thus *puñña* was regarded as an inferior form of good conduct motivated by mundane desires. In fact, as one advanced to the level of religious spiritual awareness, the aim of attaining *puñña* for a happy rebirth had to be renounced in favour of the nonworldly *Brahmacariya* conduct. The following is an example of such a view:

Herein he who has transcended both good [*puñña*] and bad and the ties as well, who is sorrowless, stainless and pure, him I call a brāhmaṇa.

Dhammapada verse 412[6]

Another such example is found in the *Saṃyutta Nikāya* recorded to have taken place at the time the Brahmin beggar Bhikkhaka asked the Buddha what the difference was between the two of them since both engaged in begging. The historical Buddha replied:

No man is rightly a 'beggar' insofar as he merely seeks alms from others. If one hold evil dharma and begs from others he does not thereby become a bhikku. Whoever in this world renounces virtue [*puñña*] and evil [*pāpa*], practicing religious goodness [*Brahmacariya*], and goes through the world with profound thinking, that person is a bhikku.[7]

25

Thus *puñña* is clearly an inferior form of good conduct since the motivation for acquiring it was considered impure.

From the position of the monk, the practice of *puñña* was viewed primarily as related to laymen. For instance, in the *Majjhima Nikāya*, the story is told of how a monk who had entered the Sangha against the wishes of his parents later returned to visit them. At that time the parents entreated him to return to the laity by saying, "My beloved child, if you are at home you can create *puñña* by your offerings." To such a temptation the monk replied, "I am not practicing the *Brahmacariya* for heavenly maidens (*accharā*)."[8] This pun denotes how clearly related the concept of *puñña* was with the desire for heaven.

Even though *puñña* was specifically meant for the laymen, the monks did not totally neglect its practice. It was an obstacle for them only insofar as its ultimate goal represented a form of worldly happiness. If the monk could practice *puñña* without any desire to obtain a happy rebirth, then he could acquire further forms of merit.[9]

The main practice of *puñña* was *dāna* (offering) but in its broadest sense, *dāna* was never meant to merely represent material offerings to the Buddhist Sangha. It referred to all the types of offering an individual could contribute to others and to society:

> Say of what folk by day and night
> For ever doth the merit [*puñña*] grow?
> In righteousness and virtuous might
> What folk from earth to heaven go?

> Planters of groves and fruitful trees,
> And they who build causeway and dam,
> And wells construct and watering-sheds
> And (to the homeless) shelter give: —
> Of such as these by day and night
> For ever doth the merit grow.
> In righteousness and virtue's might
> Such folk from earth to heaven go.[10]

In this respect, the practice of *dāna* referred to all the types of conduct that would benefit others.

The *Sīla* or morality for the laity consisted of the prohibitions against killing, stealing, lying, drinking and sexual indulgence.[11] And the promise of rebirth in a happy heaven was not the only inducement for the layman to seek to acquire *puñña*, for the threat of the hells was also present.

Unwholesome karma (*akusala kamma*) was considered to be the antithesis of *puñña* and such a form of karma was only considered to occur at the worldly level. There was no form of unwholesome karma at the level of religious conduct, for once a monk committed a transgression he was no longer observing religious conduct. The contrast between *puñña* and evil conduct can clearly be seen in the early texts:

All must die. Life is death. They shall go according to their karma, following the result of virtue [*puñña*] and evil [*pāpa*]. Because of evil karma to hell [*niraya*] and because of virtuous karma to the good place [*suggati*]. Thus one should do good [*kalyāṇa*] which is accumulating a fortune for the future.[12]

Basically, *puñña* and *pāpa* refer respectively to the purification and defilement of the mind. This is why they were believed to lead the individual to happy or miserable future states. As Dhammapāla, the famous commentator has explained, *puñña* means "cleansing the continuation"[13] which refers to karma in its broadest sense as human life or the sum total of human actions. *Puñña* begins the process of mental purification which ultimately leads the practitioner to an understanding of religious truths. The final goal of the monks was Nirvana, a psychological attitude, and the attainment of this goal could only be achieved by properly conditioning the mind. This was the ultimate aim of the teaching for the laity. The concept of hell (*niraya* or *naraka*) was thus used as a deterrent to actions that would create a mental attitude in opposition to Nirvana or Enlightenment.

## B. *Naraka and the Principal Doctrines of Early Buddhism*

The fundamental doctrine of Early Buddhism was the theory of *Paṭicca-samuppāda* (Interdependent Origination), which in effect can be said to represent the essence of the historical Buddha's Enlightenment. Out of this basic teaching, concepts such as non-self (*anattā*), the transitory nature of the world (*anicca*), karma and the teaching of the Four Noble Truths were all natural by-products.

Although it is possible to apply the theory of *Paṭicca-samuppāda* to all phenomena, this was not the original intention of the historical Buddha who was concerned with man and human suffering. Attempts to explain the nature or composition of the universe were deemed valid insofar as they contributed to the alleviation of human suffering.

Suffering (*dukkha*) as it was known in Early Buddhism, was a far more generalized term than we understand it to be in modern usage. The Early Buddhist concept of 'suffering' included all our general notions of physical and psychological pain and frustration as well as more subtle and less obvious sufferings. The realization that pleasures and happiness are not lasting, that man is finite and mortal, all of these are regarded to be forms of suffering. Even the higher stages of religious meditation entailed suffering because of their impermanence.[14] Generally, all of these forms of suffering were symbolized under the heading of "birth and death" with death representing the supreme suffering for man, casting its shadow over all the events of his life, constantly reminding him that he is finite, his pleasures must end, his wealth and power are temporary, and that eventually he will succumb to the decay and infirmities of sickness and old age.

The Buddhists logically attributed the cause of human suffering to birth[15] since it was obvious that these sufferings stemmed from the fact man was *human*. In other words, they were deemed to be natural by-products of the human condition. The symbolic compound that encompassed the entire realm of human longings and sufferings was thus expressed as "birth and death."

When the historical Buddha analyzed the sufferings encompassed

28

under the title of "birth and death," he reached the conclusion that these were the result of a psychological state of mind, which he termed "ignorance" (Pa. *avijjā*). Birth, the temporary nature of happiness, old age and death are actually events producing a minimum of physical pain. They produce suffering because of the individual's own egocentric desire (*taṇhā*) to be that which he is not — a god-like entity possessing eternal youth, immortality and enduring pleasures. Refusal to accept even a single reality of life leads to human suffering. Although the average individual will admit to himself that he is mortal and must eventually succumb to old age, this does not necessarily stop him from the search for some form of immortality and some lasting objects to cling to amidst the uncertainties of life. Even the slightest such attempt is doomed to failure and frustration. Thus the Buddhists were able to say that "birth and death" are a result of ignorance — or man's failure to understand his true situation.

In Early Buddhism the relationship between ignorance and suffering was set forth in the twelve links of *Paṭicca-samuppāda* which analyzes the life of ignorant man in the following manner:[16]

1) *Through ignorance (avijjā) arise the conditioned volitional actions;*

Ignorance represents the lack of understanding of the nature of human reality and in particular of the working of *Paṭicca-samuppāda* in the life of ignorant men. This ignorance gives rise to human actions.

2) *Through volitional actions (sankhāra) is conditioned consciousness;*

The volitional actions arising out of ignorance can be classified as:
  mental *sankhāra* — thirst, anger, stupidity, etc.
  vocal *sankhāra* — lies, needless chatter, speaking ill of others, etc.
  physical *sankhāra* — killing, stealing, sexual indulgence, etc.

These *sankhāra* are identical with karma. Every action leaves an indelible mark and it has been the moment to moment accumulation of past actions that has created the abilities, personality and character of the present individual. Since these actions have arisen from ignorance, their results are tinted by ignorance and these are deposited within the consciousness.

3) *Through consciousness (viññāna) are conditioned mental and physical phenomena or individuality;*

Consciousness in this instance can be considered from two aspects:

a) As the function of organ awareness —
   eye-consciousness, touch-consciousness, etc. and in the case of the sixth organ, which in Buddhism is the mind, the mental acts such as decision, imagination, understanding and so on.
b) as a collective body —
   In which case consciousness acts as the accumulation of past experience.

These two meanings of consciousness work together in unison. For instance, we can take the case of the awareness of a burning match. The eye-consciousness and touch-consciousness transmit this awareness to the mind where it is identified and classified in accordance with the accumulation of past experience. It is remembered that fire burns the fingers and the mind transmits the decision to the hand to extinguish the match. In the case of the ignorant man, his past experience has accumulated karma derived from the fulfillment of egocentric desires and thus his judgment is warped and often the decision is erroneous. He sees and evaluates all objects in relation to his false understanding of reality.

Under no circumstances is this form of consciousness to be considered as an independent entity and it works in an inseparable relationship with mental and physical phenomena.

4) *Through mental and physical phenomena or individuality (nāma-rūpa) are conditioned the six faculties;*
5) *Through the six faculties (saḷāyatana) is conditioned contact;*

Although the twelve links of *Paṭicca-samuppāda* arise in close union and cannot be regarded in a manner of chronological sequence, we find that these two factors and mind are particularly united. Mental and physical phenomena or individuality can be viewed from two different aspects:

a) objects of consciousness —
Referring to all that the six faculties take to be their objects. This includes exterior phenomena as well as the mental objects of consciousness.
b) product of consciousness —
Just as consciousness accumulates past experiences and actions, so the present individual represents the product of this accumulation.

Actually both of these aspects are identical insofar as the individual is created as the result of the objects of his consciousness, i.e., the present character and personality are the result of past actions, environment, what others think of the individual, his assigned social identity and so on.

Even the present condition of the physical body is a result of food assimilated and living environment. The six faculties (organs) present the transmission of exterior sensations to the mind as well as physical objects.

6) *Through contact (phassa) is conditioned sensation;*

The situation where mind, objects and faculties (organs) come into contact and begin to function.

7) *Through sensation (vedanā) is conditioned thirst or desire;*

Sensations represent the resulting pain or comfort arising from such physical and mental functioning, which in this case are based upon ignorance. Actually, there are three different varieties of sensation consisting of: suffering, joy and neutral types. All sensations are dependent upon the mind and are products of past experience as well as mental conditioning. It is therefore quite possible for two different people to receive opposite sensations from the same object. Such sensations ultimately arouse the desires.

8) *Through desire (taṇhā) is conditioned clinging;*

The raw result of sensations based upon the accumulation of experience. Pleasant situations are sought while pain and discomfort are avoided.

9) *Through clinging (upādāna) is conditioned the process of becoming;*

Discrimination applied to raw desires selecting the objects to be sought after and those to be avoided. Such clinging ultimately leads to the becoming of a new personality.

10) *Through the process of becoming (bhava) is conditioned birth;*

As a result of the foregoing desires and clinging, the process of creating a new personality begins. The circle of thirst and clinging formed the basis of the present personality and also create the fundamental pattern to influence the future.

11) *Through birth (jāti) are conditioned* 12) *old age and death (jarāmaraṇa)*

The development of the new personality based upon the foregoing desires and clinging is born. The sufferings that in turn arise out of this new personality lead to an increase of ignorance and repetition of the entire cycle.

Thus these twelve links compose a circular chain with no

beginning and no end. We can summarize this in the following

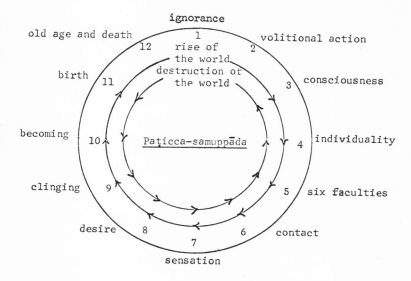

Because of ignorance, man experiences the suffering entailed by birth and death but at the same time, because of his very existence as man, he falls prey to ignorance, which his sufferings merely serve to increase. The nature of this vicious circle is well expressed in the parable of the arrow found in the *Saṃyutta Nikāya*.[17] Here it is explained how both ignorant and Enlightened men are capable of experiencing pleasantness, pain and neutral feelings but there is a great difference in the method of experiencing these. For instance, if the ignorant man is struck by a single arrow, he ends up bearing the thrust of more than one shaft. The first arrow that he receives is the physical blow itself, but on top of that his ignorance leads him to feel the pain of a number of mental arrows such as agitation over who shot him, the desire for revenge, concern over the seriousness of his wound and so forth. In fact, before he is through he has suffered from the effect of a countless number of mental and psychological arrows that have been added to the pain of the initial wound itself. The Enlightened One on the other hand, does not receive the impact of these mental and psychological arrows but merely suffers the physical pain of the first arrow itself. The moral of this story demonstrates the fact that human beings suffer more from their own psychological attitudes than from actual physical sufferings. This is the source of the vicious circle between ignorance and 'birth and death.'

When the teaching of *Paṭicca-samuppāda* is summed up in a brief formula it is stated as:

> When this is, that comes to be
> When this arises, that arises,
> When this is not, that does not come to be,
> When this ceases, that ceases.[18]

Based upon such a view, the Early Buddhists could speak of the arise of human suffering in the form of birth and death as the 'rise of the world' (*lokassa samudaya*) and the destruction of human suffering as the 'destruction of the world' (*lokassa atthangama*).[19] Such terms do not refer to the objective world as such but merely to the world of individual human ignorance, which was their principal concern. Enlightenment alone could break through the circle and bring release from 'birth and death' or from the effects of human suffering engendered by the improper psychological attitude towards life.

The doctrine of *Paṭicca-samuppāda* can be also applied to phenomena in order to emphasize the impermanent and transitory nature of all existents but this was not the major concern of the Early Buddhists.[20] When they spoke of the 'world' they were thinking in terms of the individual subjective world and the individual needs in order to attain Enlightenment; they were not interested in producing an objective world theory as such.[21] Each individual was believed to create his own 'world' as a product of his mental attitude and it was this 'world' that the Buddhists interpreted as the working ground for salvation. The so-called exterior objective world was of minor significance and only a proper object of Buddhist concern when it might affect individual

34

Enlightenment.[22] For instance, in the case where humans conceive the erroneous notion that material objects are desirable independent entities with permanent natures, then it is necessary to apply the doctrine of *Paticca-samuppāda* to the exterior world in order to correct this false view.

In applying *Paticca-samuppāda* to the individual, the primary concern of the Early Buddhists was the relationship between ignorance and suffering, while at the same time the theory also demonstrated how man is a temporary product of multiple direct and indirect conditions with no underlying soul or essence (*attā*). Applied to the human container world, the theory demonstrated the impermanent, interdependent nature of all phenomena.

One of the major causes of human suffering was deemed to be the natural desire to cling to that which appears to be real and unchangeable; to find joys that are lasting and finally to perpetuate individual life itself. When this cannot be realized, suffering inevitably results. The Buddhists termed this 'clinging' (*upādāna*), which is based upon desire (*taṇhā*), and is the product of ignorance (*avijjā*). Although primarily this is an egotistical desire or an attachment to the self, at times it even assumes religious forms such as seeking a permanent abode in an after-life. For all ages of Buddhists, even Nirvana is considered to be a temporary condition subject to rise and decay, and it is believed that as long as man enjoys a human body he will never find a permanent state of repose.[23] On the other hand, once the human body is destroyed, 'man' as such, no longer exists.

In Early Buddhism the concept of karma closely interacted with the doctrine of *Paticca-samuppāda*. This is particularly obvious in the relationship between volitional actions (*sankhāra*) and consciousness (*viññāṇa*). Karma (derived from *kr̥*, "to act") can be defined in Early Buddhist philosophy as the function of life of physical and mental actions based upon the human will.[24] This was quite a different concept from the fatalistic view popular among certain segments of the masses. The belief in *Paticca-samuppāda* completely negated the idea that there existed any enduring substance within the human being that could literally reincarnate into another life. At the same time, it even denied that there existed any permanent entity lasting through the present human life. Man was viewed as a product of changing interrelated conditions and it was in this respect that birth could be said to occur at every moment. As the historical Buddha once stated, "When the Aggregates arise, decay and die, O Monk, every moment you are born, decay and die."[25] The one common thread of continuity running from 'existence' to 'existence' was believed to be karma. Psychological and even physical features may change, as in the movement from child to adult, but the actions created along the way condition each step of change in the process. It can even be said that karma represents human life itself as the sum total of actions and interactions.

Karma makes its influence felt upon human life by conditioning consciousness from one birth (existence) to the next. For example, we can notice how the quality of consciousness changes in our daily life resulting from the influence of our actions since mind and action are interrelated. It is in this respect that the mind is described as the accumulation of actions and experiences of the past. By means of such accumulation the contents of individual minds differ. The artist, as a result of his past training (actions) and experience has created the mind of an artist, just as the merchant develops the mind of a merchant. This does not mean that one cannot change, but if he does that change itself is a result of actions and experience. An endless circle is created by this accumulation of past knowledge and experience that influences the present actions (or karma) which in turn influence the future. Thus the Early Buddhists could say that "by *avijjā* (ignorance), there exists *sankhāra* (action), and because of *sankhāra,* there exists *viññāna* (consciousness)." In such a context human sufferings, represented as 'birth and death,' all lead to the contents of the human mind. Thus, although the karma of the past does not directly determine the present state of joy or suffering, it does influence it indirectly by means of interaction with the mind. For example, a modern man can experience joy in receiving a large amount of money since in the past his mind has been conditioned to appreciate the value of money. If he were to present the same sum to his ancestors of three thousand years ago, it would appear to be a form of useless trash. In this respect, the mind assumes the position of mediator between actions (karma) and the experience of joy and suffering. This in turn creates an endless circle:

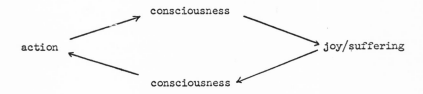

In view of the power or influence exerted by karma upon consciousness, it can be said that at any given moment the individual's psychological attitude is either the direct or indirect result of his karma. Good (*kusala*) and bad (*akusala*) karma in this case would relate to the mental states produced — either freedom from suffering or the inducement of suffering. Symbolically the individual is chained by his egocentric desires or attachment to self, and the bad karma generated as the result of this greed leads him to be 'born' into the realm of suffering or hell (*naraka*). In other words, his present mental attitude has been conditioned by his past actions in which he allowed his desires to control him. This has been stated in the *Dhammapada* in the following manner:

> Mind foreruns (all evil) conditions, mind is chief
> mind made are they; if one speaks or acts with
> wicked mind, because of that, pain pursues him,
> even as the wheel following the hoof of the draught ox.[26]

> The craving of the person addicted to careless living
> grows like a creeper; he jumps from life to life
> like a fruit-loving monkey in the forest.[27]

On the other hand, the individual reaping the reward of good actions enjoys an easier state of mind in the present since he is not so dominated by ignorance and desire. His level of existence can be described symbolically as representing the deva heavens, realms of relative peace and tranquility. In later Abhidharma Buddhism these psychological states were more fully explored and related to the Three World (*ti-loka*) theory.

The aim of the religious in Early Buddhism was to attain a mental attitude completely free of egotistical desires (*taṇhā*). In other words, to break the entire chain of ignorance and be freed from re-birth. As the historical Buddha reportedly exclaimed upon his Enlightenment:

> Through many a birth I wandered in saṃsāra
> seeking, but not finding, the builder of the house.
> Sorrowful is birth again and again.
> O House-builder! Thou art seen. Thou shalt
> build no house again. All thy rafters are
> broken, thy ridge-pole is shattered.
> My mind has attained the unconditioned,
> achieved is the end of cravings.[28]

He discovered that egocentric desire, the product of his own mental state, created his house of suffering which was supported by the ridge-pole of ignorance. By shattering this ignorance, he attained freedom from the endless round of rebirths and reached Nirvana.

When the Enlightened One speaks of having conquered birth and death, it symbolically refers to overcoming suffering; it does not mean that he has ceased to be a product of constantly changing conditions. He has merely destroyed the world of human sufferings or the circle of *Paṭicca-samuppāda* as it describes the existence of the ignorant man. In the same respect, it is said that the Enlightened One has become freed of karma. This does not mean that his actions no longer have any result, but rather that the result is outside the circle of ignorance and 'birth and death.' Since his mental state of ignorance has been completely overcome, now his actions can only lead him on to higher and purer mental conditions. The new circle becomes a round of purification and increasing freedom. In Early Buddhism the first step towards becoming an Arahant or Enlightened One was termed 'Entering the Stream' *(sotāpatti-magga)*. Symbolically, such an individual can be viewed as one who has overcome the ignorant compulsion to struggle against the realities of life and finally entered the harmonious current to flow towards increasing happiness. It also represents the individual liberated from the depths of his own mental hell to climb the heavenly heights of peace and serenity.

## C. *Early Buddhist Cosmology and Descriptions of Naraka*

Although the Early Buddhists sought to avoid world speculation *(loka cintā)*,[29] they did absorb many of the beliefs of contemporary Indian society regarding the nature of the physical universe and these were later systematized by the Abhidharma schools. The general belief was that Mt. Sumeru formed the center of the world surrounded by four great islands *(dīpa)* or continents amongst which Jambudīpa (Skt. Jambudvīpa) on the south represented India. The early Pāli texts contain very few references to the physical universe.[30] In place of developing an interest in the nature of the exterior world, the Early Buddhists were concerned with a spiritual cosmology that was used to serve two purposes: the first, as an *upāya* to induce the layman to practice virtue, and the second, as a representation of the various stages and potentialities of human consciousness. This psychocosmic universe was divided into three 'worlds' consisting of *Kāma loka* (the world of desire), *Rūpa loka* (world of form) and *Arūpa loka* (world of non-form). Each so-called world was further divided into various realms or stages whose names were mostly borrowed from the Indian cosmology.[31] The *Rūpa* and *Arūpa loka* were correlated to the higher stages of Buddhist meditation leading towards the ultimate goal of Nirvana, which was still considered to be beyond these three worlds of birth and death. *Kāma loka* or the world of desire dealt more closely with the daily psychological possibilities of man and was divided into Five Realms *(gati)* or Existences consisting of:[32]

1) The Hells — Niraya or Naraka
2) Realm of Animals — Tiracchāna-yoni
3) Realm of Unfulfilled Desires or Hungry Ghosts — Petti-visaya
4) Human Realm — Manussa
5) Realms of the Deva Heavens — Deva loka

Used as an *upāya* for the laity, these worlds served as the inducement to practice virtue in order to obtain future rebirth in a pleasant realm and to avoid the sufferings of the hells. Even at this level, however, the realms were all understood to exist within the cycle of birth and death and could never represent permanent places of repose.

Although the early texts are not explicit in explaining how the Five Existences were meant to be interpreted as potentialities of consciousness, their symbolism is quite apparent. The realms of the deva heavens would encompass the purer more spiritual stages of man and the higher elements of human civilization such as art, music, philosophy and so on. The realm of man would relate to the life of reason and logic. The realms of animals and hungry ghosts respectively would deal with instinctive behaviour and mental states dominated by greed and avarice, while the hells would represent the enmeshed webs of suffering accumulating from past actions (karma) that induce further suffering and temptations. To interpret such psychological potentialities within the sphere of a contemporary day, we can take for example the situation of a businessman who spends his morning engaged in cutthroat competition with his business colleagues (hells); at noon he overeats while worrying how to make more money (both in the realm of hungry ghosts); following which he falls prey to instinctive sensual desires (animal). Later in the day he regrets his past actions and exercises control over his behaviour (man) and finally in the evening he goes to attend a musical concert (deva). Thus in the course of one day any individual can easily move through all Five Realms of Existence.

The Early Buddhists were not content with mere symbols for the hells but also attempted to provide names and describe vivid tortures. The latter were particularly useful as means of instructing the laity. The hells were not yet systematized at this time and we find the earliest texts enumerate ten niraya consisting of:[33]

1) Abbuda
2) Nirabbuda
3) Ababa
4) Ahaha
5) Aṭaṭa
6) Kumuda (Yellow Lotus)
7) Sogandhika (White water lily)
8) Uppalaka (Blue Lotus)
9) Puṇḍarīka (White Lotus)
10) Paduma (Red Lotus)

The significance of these names is not clear. Some commentators believed they merely represented time spans of what was later known as the Avīci (No-interval) hell although this term was not used in the Nikāyas to refer to hell.[34]

The *Aṅguttara Nikāya* presents a distinct picture of the nature of the sufferings that undoubtedly served as a useful *upāya* for those whose religious awareness was not sufficiently aroused to lead a virtuous life for its own rewards.[35] In this account a judgment by Yama, the Lord of Death is described. After first questioning the sinner why he has failed to heed the messengers of old age, sickness and death, Yama then sends him to suffer for his negligence where:

1) First he is tortured with the five-fold pinion, by which hot iron stakes are driven through his hands, feet and chest;
2) He is laid down and planed with adzes;
3) Next he is planed with razors;

41

4) The demons bid him to a chariot and drive him up and down over the burning ground;
5) He is pushed up a huge burning mountain of red hot coal;
6) He is tossed into a burning brass caldron where he is cooked as he bobs up and down in the boiling mass;

Finally, after these initial tortures, he is tossed into a great square hell composed of iron walls, ceiling and floor with four iron doors. At times each of the doors of this great hell open, but just as the sinner is about to escape, it slams shut again. At length, after the end of a long period, once again the east door opens and the sinner escapes. Outside of the great hell he now encounters the sufferings of the minor hells:[36]

1) He falls into the hell of dung *(gūtha)* where needle beaked worms rip away his skin and flesh, devouring even the marrow of his bones;
2) Next he stumbles into the burning coal hell *(kukkuḷa);*
3) After which he enters the forest of silk cotton trees *(simbalivana)* with sharp thorns all ablaze, and he is forced to climb the trees;
4) Next he encounters the Great Sword-leaf forest *(asipattavana)* where he is sliced to shreds whenever the wind stirs;
5) Finally, he tumbles into a bitter river *(khārodhaka)* where he bobs up and down while the demons try to catch him with a fish hook. When they do catch him they ask him what he desires and as soon as he replies that he is thirsty they proceed to pour molten copper into his mouth to course through his entire body.

After all of these torments, the demons toss the sinner back into the Great Hell to repeat the entire process over again. There can be no end to suffering until the evil karma that the sinner himself has created can be burnt up or exhausted. Thus even at this level of symbolic explanation, it is clear that individuals must

42

reap the sufferings that they have caused for themselves. Once this retribution is exacted, they are freed from suffering.

### D. *Hell in Abhidharma Buddhism*

Approximately one hundred years after the death of the historical Buddha, the Buddhist sangha experienced a major division into conservative and liberal groups followed by numerous subdivisions. Over the span of nearly four hundred years, twenty Buddhist groups came into existence. These were the so-called twenty Hīnayāna schools and this period is known as Abhidharma Buddhism.[37] Each of these schools compiled and transmitted its own set of sacred scriptures and they also created numerous philosophical treatises that have come to be known as the Abhidharma piṭaka. Primarily the purpose of these texts was to gather various doctrines found in the sutras and to arrange them systematically. Such an effort was initially necessary to clarify the tenets of Buddhist theology, but eventually it strayed into the realm of mere philosophical speculation. Abstract concepts began to assume tangible form and particularly in dealing with the hells or *narakas,* we can observe this change of orientation. The Abhidharma scholars continued to use the theory of the three worlds in their psychological treatises as potentialities of human consciousness and made considerable contributions in this area to the development of Buddhist psychology but they also sought to understand the theory as an explanation for the composition of the physical universe. For instance, in the hands of the Abhidharma scholars, the *narakas* receive a geographical position, width, depth and other exact specifications. Even the life-spans of these hells were calculated. To illustrate, one of the leading Abhidharma texts, the *Mahāvibhāṣā* presents the following description of *naraka*:[38]

Below the surface of Jambudvīpa, where man resides, there is 500 yojana[39] of earth, followed by 500 yojana of white earth and 19,000 yojana composing seven of the hells. The width of these hells is 10,000 yojana each and below them is located an Eighth and final hell which is 20,000 yojana deep and square.

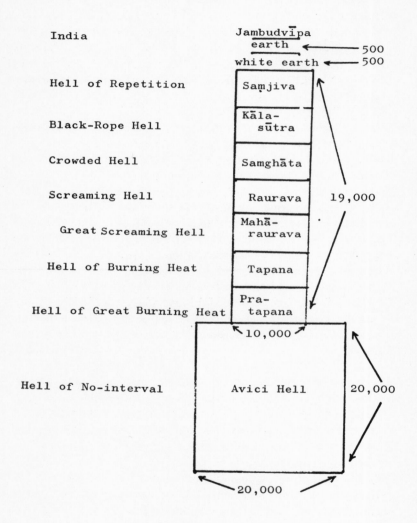

India        Jambudvīpa
earth     ←     500
white earth ←   500

Hell of Repetition      Saṃjiva

Black-Rope Hell      Kāla-sūtra

Crowded Hell      Samghāta

Screaming Hell      Raurava      19,000

Great Screaming Hell      Mahā-raurava

Hell of Burning Heat      Tapana

Hell of Great Burning Heat      Pra-tapana

10,000

Hell of No-interval      Avici Hell      20,000

20,000

44

The *Abhidharmakośa,* of the same period presented a time span for the various hells based upon the time spans of the six various deva heavens.[40] To illustrate, the following life-spans were calculated for the heavens:

| *Human years to equal one day* | | *Life-span of heaven* |
|---|---|---|
| 50 | Heaven of Four Deva Kings | 500 years |
| 100 | Trāyastriṃśa | 1,000 years |
| 200 | Yāma Heaven | 2,000 years |
| 400 | Tusita | 4,000 years |
| 800 | Nirmāṇarati Heaven | 8,000 years |
| 1,600 | Paranirmita-vaśavartin | 16,000 years |

These periods formed the criteria for determining the time spans of the hells in the following manner:[41]

| *Hell* | *One day equals life-span of:* | *Life-span of Hell* |
|---|---|---|
| Samjīva | Heaven of Four Deva Kings | 500 years |
| Kāla-sūtra | Trāyastriṃśa Heaven | 1,000 years |
| Saṃghāta | Yāma Heaven | 2,000 years |
| Raurava | Tuṣita Heaven | 4,000 years |
| Mahā-raurava | Nirmāṇarati Heaven | 8,000 years |
| Tapana | Paranirmitavaśavartin | 16,000 years |
| Pratapana | —————— | half a medium kalpa |
| Avīci | —————— | medium kalpa |

The kalpa in Buddhism is calculated by two different methods. In the first, a huge forty square league cubed container is filled with mustard seed and every hundred years one seed is removed. When the container is finally empty, one small kalpa is completed. There are three degrees of kalpa: small, medium and large. A medium kalpa, as mentioned in regards to the seventh and eighth hells, uses an eighty square league container.[42]

According to a second method of calculation, a rock is used in place of mustard seed. In this case, a medium kalpa consisted of the time it took for a heavenly spirit to wear out an eighty square league rock by polishing it once every hundred years.[43]

In such a manner Abhidharma Buddhism presented complex and concrete descriptions of *naraka* and the symbolism began to be grasped as a tangible reality. We can also note that the hells are now clearly systematized into eight different varieties and levels. These names and this particular grouping were to continue throughout the history of Buddhism.

Undoubtedly the Abhidharma scholars must have initiated their endeavours to geographically define the three worlds as a form of symbolism with the understanding that this was merely another *upāya*. Ultimately however, the situation developed where the *upāya* was confused with the goal and the spirit of Buddhism was lost. It was then necessary for a dissident movement to arise and counterbalance the efforts to view abstract concepts as realities. The Mādhyamika school formed this new balance and sought to return to the spirit of Early Buddhism by declaring all existents to have a void *(śūnyatā)* nature. This new movement also clarified the meaning of *naraka* from the standpoint of individual salvation.

# CHAPTER III

# HELL IN MAHĀYĀNA BUDDHISM

Generally, the distinction between "Mahāyāna" (lit. Great Vehicle) and "Hīnayāna" (deficient vehicle) Buddhism can be viewed from two different approaches; first, as geographical designations and secondly, as philosophical terms. Although the term "Hīnayāna" was originally created as a pejorative by the Mahāyānists, in modern times the distinction has become primarily geographical, referring to the varieties of Buddhism transmitted to the northern Asian countries in contrast to that disseminated in the south. The terms originally developed from the split in the Buddhist sangha occurring 100 years after the death of the historical Buddha but the major dividing issues and groups of that time have long since faded away.[1] The original division was between the conservative Sthiravadins and liberal Mahāsanghikas but successive generations witnessed the splintering of both groups with the eventual disappearance of the Mahāsanghikas, who left their legacy to modern Mahāyāna Buddhism. There was a great deal of mutual influence between the various groups during the course of the next few centuries which made the original issues become more obscure. The Mahāyāna, which spread to the northern countries such as China, Tibet, Korea and Japan remains the more liberal faction as opposed to the Theravāda school of Ceylon, which is the foremost representative of Hīnayāna Buddhism. Even the Theravādins however, accept the bodhisattva ideal, which is often considered to be one of the leading characteristics of Mahāyāna Buddhism.

The second method of viewing the distinction between Mahāyāna and Hīnayāna is upon philosophical grounds which takes us back to the original reason for the designation "Hīnayāna." By the first century B.C. when the Mahāyāna texts were being composed, Abhidharma Buddhism was flourishing and many extreme positions were developing. No doubt it appeared to many idealists that these scholar-priests were merely concerned with their own study and personal salvation, no longer having any interest in attempting to lead the masses to Enlightenment. From this standpoint, the distinction refers to the new emphasis upon universal Enlightenment and the belief that the Enlightened One cannot merely enjoy the fruits of his endeavours but that the very function of Enlightenment necessitates efforts to assist others in the attainment of the same goal. In the *Saddharma Puṇḍarīka sūtra* such criticism is directed towards a group of 5,000 religious and laymen who, believing they are already Enlightened, feel no need to listen to the Buddha's more profound teachings.[2] In other words, it was a rebuke against the pride and self-righteousness of these members. Actually, throughout the history of Buddhism all the various schools have placed emphasis upon altruism and the propagation of the teachings to benefit the laity in such a manner that strictly speaking "Hīnayāna" as popularly defined, never existed.[3] The quarrel of the so-called Mahāyānists was with the extreme elements of the scholastic Abhidharma schools and not with the entire tradition in itself.[4] If such a great division had actually taken place, it would have been impossible for the two groups to flourish side by side, often in the same monasteries, for generations.[5]

The fundamental principles of Mahāyāna Buddhism were established by the *Prajñāpāramitā sūtras,* which were first composed in the second century B.C. One of the main doctrines set forth in these sutras was the concept that all phenomena are void. (Skt. *śūnyatā*) because they are caused interdependently in accordance with the doctrines of Interdependent Origination (Skt. *Pratītya samutpāda)*. Between the period of 100 B.C. and 200 A.D. a profusion of sutras came forth with similar concepts, and these were finally systematized into a logical and philosophical form by the Mādhyamika school of Buddhism. The founder of this school, Nāgārjuna (ca. 2nd cent. A.D.) is generally considered by northern Buddhists to have been the principal founder of Mahāyāna Buddhism since his philosophy became the basis for all the various Mahāyāna schools.

## A. *Nāgārjuna and the Mādhyamika View of Human Existence*

Although Nāgārjuna, the founder of Mādhyamika philosophy, set forth a dialectic in order to combat the excesses of Abhidharma scholasticism, he did not have any intention of merely engaging in philosophical debate. Both in the opening and closing of his famous *Mūlamadhyamakakārikās*, he clearly announced his devotion to the historical Buddha, founder of the true teaching and first proclaimer of the doctrine of Interdependent Origination *(Pratītya samutpāda)*.[6] Just as this doctrine had originally represented the essence of the historical Buddha's Enlightenment, so Nāgārjuna made it the cornerstone of his philosophy believing that by so doing, he could restore the original spirit of Buddhism and counteract the extremes of Abhidharma. On the basis of *Pratītya samutpāda*, Nāgārjuna proceeded to prove that all existents were mutually dependent and devoid of any lasting or unchangeable core or essence. Because of this theory, he believed that the worldly objects which humans commonly cling to and believe to represent reality are in truth void *(śūnyatā)*; insofar as they are all dependent upon causes and conditions, consequently incapable of self-subsistence. The test of "reality" to Nāgārjuna was always self-subsistence and since no existent possessed this quality, all were declared empty or void *(śūnyatā)*. Just as the historical Buddha had first devised a middle path between hedonism and asceticism, so Nāgārjuna sought a philosophical middle path (Mādhyamika — lit. meaning "followers of the middle") avoiding the extreme of Abhidharma realism or the error of nihilism;

thereby returning to what he believed was the spirit of Early Buddhism.

Although Nāgārjuna spent a great deal of time setting forth his dialectical arguments to prove the void (śūnyatā) nature of all phenomena, the basis of his interest actually was related to the problems of human existence. Primarily he visualized these as arising from the improper understanding of the relationship between human consciousness (vijñāna) and the objects of the outer world (nāma-rūpa). Unfortunately, western interpreters of his philosophy have tended to be more interested in his philosophical arguments and dialectic than the religious basis of his work. The following is an interpretation of Nāgārjuna's view of actual human existence.

Human consciousness (vijñāna) functions upon the so-called world (nāma-rūpa) by grasping this world in order to affirm its own existence. "Self" is differentiated from "other" and the propensity (vāsanā) arises to cling to this "self" as an absolute and to "others" as attributes possessed by the "self."[7] From such a mental attitude the common notions of "I am" and "this is mine" issue forth with "self" (ātman) feeding upon the outer world, just as fire upon firewood,[8] in order to nourish its illusion of being an absolute. As a result of this natural human tendency to cling to self and property, possessions and loved ones in the outer world, a veritable snowball of ignorance is created that inevitably leads to suffering and frustration. The events of human life constantly thwart the individual self's desires to be an absolute and the objects that he seeks to possess in order to prove his own permanence constantly are undergoing change and destruction until in the end he is left grasping merely their empty hulls. He moves from goal to goal, from seeking to be loved, to the acquisition of wealth and power but in the end nothing is lasting. All, including the self, finally fades away into the oblivion of time. In such a situation, the ignorant man is like a child trying to catch and preserve the fragile beauty of the falling snowflakes and ultimately destined to the tears of frustration.

In contrast to the false illusion created by human subjectivity, Nāgārjuna viewed the true relationship between the subject or "self" and its objects to be an interdependent relationship (*Pratītya samutpāda*), functioning in the same manner as fire and firewood:

> Fire does not exist in relation to kindling;
> and fire does not exist *un*related to kindling.
> Kindling does not exist in relation to fire;
> and kindling does not exist *un*related to fire.[9]

In other words, the relationship is one of mutual dependency and neither the fire nor firewood stand alone as independent entities. In the same manner, human subjectivity and its objects are considered to be mutually dependent upon each other. The individual is interrelated with his fellow men and environment and must necessarily function in harmony rather than seek to suit his own egocentric desires.

In analyzing the basis of human existence, Nāgārjuna viewed the doctrine of *Pratītya samutpāda* from the standpoint of the rise and destruction of human existence. The rise of human existence (*pravṛtti naya*), according to this view begins with the factors of consciousness (*vijñāna*) and material objects (*nāma-rūpa*), which constitute beginning portions of the famous twelve links of *Pratītya samutpāda*. The destruction of human existence (*nivṛtti naya*) commences with the last of the links, consisting of old age and death (*jarāmarana*). Following this formula, Nāgārjuna visualized human ignorance (*avidyā*) to be the source of separation between the subjective self and outer world. It is this ignorance, the product of discriminative knowledge, that creates the illusion of an absolute self, which in reality does not exist. Once this illusion is shattered, then the common sense view of human existence no longer can exist for:

> If the individual self does not exist, how
> then will there be something which is 'my
> own'? . . . He who is without possessiveness and
> who has no ego- He, also, does not exist. . .
> When 'I' and 'mine' have stopped, then also

51

there is not an outside nor an inner self.
The 'acquiring' [of karma] (*upādāna*) has
stopped; on account of that destruction,
there is destruction of very existence.[10]

This does not actually mean that the individual ceases to physically exist, but merely that he ceases to exist in the cycle of ignorance where he believed that he was an absolute entity and thus grasped the objects in the world about him. With the destruction of this ignorant common sense existence, the vicious circle leading to ceaseless frustration and suffering is also broken and the individual attains his freedom. The method to achieve such freedom is the inner realization that an absolute self does not exist and that consciousness and its objects in the outer world are mutually dependent upon each other. Ultimately, this is merely a change of mental attitude but such a realization necessitates shattering the very foundations of normal daily life, which are based upon the discrimination between self and others, or in other words, upon categorical reasoning.

Subjective discrimination forms the very basis of daily human life since all human discourse and knowledge require such differentiation. Each object man encounters he must label and in so doing separates as being 'other' than himself. He then proceeds to evaluate these objects in terms of "self" and project his personal desires and wishes upon them. It is in such a manner that humans create their own individual worlds. Each object encountered is valued in terms of one's own personal scheme of importance. For instance, an individual may view the large maple tree in his front yard to be a valuable asset while his neighbor can only see it as an annoying nuisance ruining cement walks and dropping leaves. If the tree however should become infected with pests or suddenly threaten the owner's house, then unthinkingly he will decide to dispose of it since its value has disappeared. The entire criteria for evaluating whether the tree is desirable or not do not take into slightest consideration any possible feelings or rights of the tree itself. Such would be regarded as sentimentalism. It is in the same vein that modern man becomes interested in ecology when his own future survival appears to be threatened and only a handful of individuals are ever concerned with protecting nature for its own sake.

With such a constant discrimination between 'self' and 'other' and the ensuing projection of one's own values, it is almost totally impossible in daily life to ever view an object as-it-really-is. Constant ego distortion enters into the picture and taints everything it encounters so that the individual is only capable of judging the objects and world around him in relation to his own desires and goals.

Nāgārjuna termed the expression of human reality based upon categorical reasoning to be *prapañca*, a term originally used to describe the chatter of fools.[11] He also stated:

> *Prapañca* is the root of all contentions and
> *prapañca* is the clinging to words. The ignorant
> pursue names while what they seek is reality. They
> misapply the sense of the real; they mistake the
> specific for the ultimate, the relative for the
> absolute. In this they follow their own fancy
> instead of the nature of things as they are. Hence
> the contradictions which they meet at every step.[12]

Such distortions only lead to human suffering insofar as they encourage the individual to pursue his path of clinging to exterior objects in the vain belief that they will bring him lasting pleasure or happiness. The only release from such a world of clinging and ignorance is a true understanding of the relationship between subjectivity and the objective world in view of the law of *Pratītya samutpāda*. Such an understanding makes the individual realize that 'self' and the objective world are both mutually interdependent and that nothing can be grasped as durable or permanent since all existents, including what composes the so-called 'self' are devoid (*śūnyatā*) of independent substance. The 'self' is actually incapable of grasping since it is merely a temporary collection of Five Aggregates that are constantly undergoing change and transformation. The objects in the exterior world are undergoing the same type of change and even if the 'self', in view of its changing composition does not reject them, they will also change and cease to be the object originally acquired. Thus, although the man who chooses a beautiful woman may not tire of her, the beauty he once prized will inevitably wither and disappear. Man constantly changes and so does the world around him and it is the refusal to accept and harmonize with such changes that produces the bitterest forms of suffering. The static unchangeable world is merely an illusion created by the ego doomed to be shattered in the face of reality.

Besides realizing the *śūnyatā* nature of the subjecive self and world around us, another essential understanding is the fact that this interdependent relationship is beginningless. To make such a view clear, Nāgārjuna rejected the following as false views:

1) That subjectivity existed as an independent substance prior to the rise of objectivity, which followed to form the dependent relationship.
2) The reverse of the former, with objectivity existing prior to subjectivity.
3) That both subjectivity and objectivity initially existed as separate entities and subsequently united to form a dependent relationship.[13]

The law of *Pratītya samutpāda* denies such views and refuses to permit any form of a beginning original substance.

B. *Concept of Emptiness*

The path Nāgārjuna envisioned leading to Enlightenment was by means of realizing the interdependent nature of both the subject and object or of man and his surroundings. Such a realization would entail the cessation of clinging and acquisitiveness and

54

bring the individual back into harmony with his fellow men and environment. This is his understanding of Emptiness or *śūnyatā*; the condition where human existence can be viewed as-it-is freed from ego projections or false illusions. In other words, this is a type of absolute objectivity but it does not mean that every Enlightened person suddenly acquires some supernatural vision enabling them to view the world in an identical manner. According to the Buddhist view, each individual creates his own world, which is highly dependent upon personal karma. The blind Enlightened One does not gain the physical vision to perceive the world about him in a conventional manner but he does comprehend his relationship with his own world in a true light. In the same way, no two Enlightened individuals necessarily observe an object identically. What they both share is the ability to comprehend the objects surrounding them free from the mental or ego-centered delusions that ordinary men foster upon their environment. This is the absolute objectivity of Enlightenment or realization of *śūnyatā*. In some respects it is similar to the situation of a dying man who accepts his plight gracefully and surrenders his clinging. In such an instance the reason for his surrender is due to a realization of his own emptiness rather than the emptiness of the objects surrounding him but he can gain the ability to view the world without ego-distortion.[14] Of course for most individuals the news of recovery destroys such an insight and they immediately return to their former habits; in some instances more vehemently than ever. The proof of true Enlightenment is not to entertain such an outlook merely when facing death or an escape from the world, but while living and functioning in daily life. This is why Nāgārjuna understood the process of Enlightenment as consisting of three simultaneous inseparable aspects: *śūnyatā, śūnyatā-yām prayojanam* and *śūnyatā artha*.[15]

*Śūnyatā*, the first aspect, represents the condition where subjective clinging to the exterior world is denied and all clingings of the mind cease. This is the condition of perfect calm and serenity which Nāgārjuna described in the following manner:

'Not caused by something else,' 'peaceful,'

'not elaborated by discursive thought.'

'Indeterminate.' 'undifferentiated': such are

the characteristics of true reality (*tattva*).[16]

The barriers between 'self' and 'other' have now disappeared and the interrelated nature of all existents is intuitively comprehended. Logic and thought are temporarily suspended in favor of the intuitive faculties. But this merely represents one aspect of Enlightenment and if an individual is truly Enlightened the other two characteristics must also be present.

*Śūnyatāyām prayojanam* (the functioning of Emptiness) is the second aspect whereby the individual surrenders his natural human tendency to cling to his experience of *śūnyatā*. This is accomplished by self-reflection and represents the continual process of mental purification that is a necessary attribute for the Enlightened One. At the same time the individual surrenders the temptation to cling to Enlightenment he also is aware of the existence of other suffering sentient beings. For although he has broken his own chain of clinging and become truly a man of non-self (*anātman*) or one who recognizes the non-self nature of his own existence as well as of the world around him, he also realizes that the vicious circle of clinging must be broken for all. Automatically he comes to the aid of others to help them achieve the same realization that he has attained. For the Enlightened One this is not actually 'compassion' in our usual sense of the term, since he no longer has any conscious awareness of the separation between himself and 'others'; he still abides within the experience of undifferentiated oneness that he experienced in *śūnyatā*. 'Other' individuals are viewed much like the parts of his own body and their suffering instinctively becomes his own suffering, just as their joy is his joy. Working for others means working to liberate the greater part of himself and in this sense, it can almost be termed a supra-Selfish act from the standpoint of comprehending a supreme Self. This does not mean that the individual becomes absorbed or submerged, such as the Indian view of a Cosmic Consciousness is often understood, but rather that the individual realizes his own distinctive role in the great Self consisting of all existents, just as the hand might instinctively comprehend its relationship to the other members of the human body. It remains distinctly unique, yet is a part of the whole and has its own reaction to the general well-being or suffering of the body. This is analogous to the comprehension of the Enlightened One and his spontaneous need to assist others attain Enlightenment.

In the first aspect the individual achieved his own realization of *śūnyatā*. Now in this second aspect, comprehending his unity with others, the Enlightened One automatically makes their realization of *śūnyatā* his goal. In effect this is making the larger part of himself (what he is) experience *śūnyatā* since he so clearly comprehends the doctrine of *Pratītya samutpāda* or interrelatedness of all existents but understanding is not enough, there must also be action.

The third aspect of *śūnya* realization provides the practical ground for universal salvation and this is termed *śūnyatā artha* (practice of Emptiness in the conventional world). It is also defined as the temporal presentation of Emptiness. In other words, *śūnyatā* transcends human language, yet the Enlightened One (or bodhisattva) must seek to set forth his teaching in the language of the world. Naturally such an attempt leads to distortion but there is no other method by which he can lead his fellow men to their realization of *śūnyatā*. This is why Nāgārjuna stated:

Emptiness, having been dimly perceived, utterly destroys the
　　　　　　　　　　　　　　　　　　　slow-witted.
It is like a snake wrongly grasped or [magical] knowledge
　　　　　　　　　　　　　　　　incorrectly applied.
Therefore the mind of the ascetic [Gautama] was diverted
　　　　　　　　　　　　　from teaching the *dharma,*
Having thought about the incomprehensibility of the *dharma*
　　　　　　　　　　　　　by the stupid.[17]

Yet despite such fears the Enlightened Ones must teach and use *upāya* or 'skillful means' to lead individuals to break their own circles of human clinging and attain freedom. These doctrines that are taught cannot actually represent Absolute Truth since human language based upon discriminative knowledge and categorical reasoning is incapable of expressing Absolute Truth. These *upāya* merely contain germs of truth tailored to suit the needs of individual beings of a certain time and place and point the way for them. In this respect Buddhism as a religion cannot offer a thetic ideology to be grasped, it merely directs the individual in hope that he will eventually transcend these very teachings; which are all merely glorified forms of *prapañca*. Yet the nature of the Enlightened One is such that he must never cease to try to communicate his experience and this is why Nāgārjuna could finally say:

> To him, possessing compassion, who taught the real *dharma*
> For the destruction of all views — to him Gautama, I humbly
> offer reverence.[18]

It would be inconceivable to imagine the historical Buddha renouncing preaching, just as it is equally unimaginable that any Enlightened One would attempt to evade his spontaneous desire to aid his fellow men. Ultimately the Enlightened One is a human being and any attempt to deny or escape the actual everyday world of human affairs would in effect be proof that his Enlightenment was not authentic. This is the difference between death-bed and drug-induced spiritual realizations; the proof of their authenticity can only be tested by a return to normal life. The belief in the necessity for the validity of Enlightenment to be dependent upon the accompanying function of desiring to work for the salvation of others, is proof that Nāgārjuna's views were neither pessimistic nor nihilistic.

Keeping in mind this basic understanding of Nāgārjuna regarding the nature of human existence and Enlightenment, we can contrast his descriptions of the ideal world with the world of ignorance by means of the following diagram:

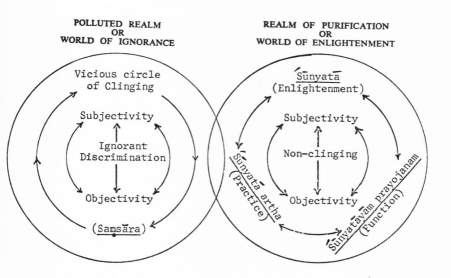

POLLUTED REALM
OR
WORLD OF IGNORANCE

REALM OF PURIFICATION
OR
WORLD OF ENLIGHTENMENT

Vicious circle
of Clinging

Subjectivity

Ignorant
Discrimination

Objectivity

(Saṃsāra)

Śūnyatā
(Enlightenment)

Subjectivity

Non-clinging

Objectivity

Śūnyatā artha
(Practice)

Śūnyatāyām prayojanam
(Function)

From this view, the soteriological nature of the Polluted Land becomes evident. Interpreting this as being equivalent to Naraka (hell) in the broadest sense, we have evidence of its dynamic nature. Just as the Realm of Purification represents the three-fold functioning of the circle of *Sūnyatā*, so the Polluted Land or hell is based upon the circle of subject-object clinging. It is the daily world where the individual self reigns supreme and all decisions and value judgments are made in accordance with the desires of this self to create its own small world of lasting happiness. Since it is based upon an illusion, it brings suffering and frustration, which in effect make it hell. For most individuals such a source of suffering is incomprehensible since they seemingly are asking for so little; a small amount of love, a little security and perhaps a delay in the aging process. Yet the little they ask is often as impossible to obtain as the great requests for riches and immortality. For Buddhists, all clinging leads to suffering be it great or small since clinging runs counter to the harmonious flow of life. Everything must be accepted with an open hand and allowed to slip away from the same. This is the simplest method of expressing the difference between the psychological sufferings of hell and the enjoyment of bliss. On the other hand, it is a mistake to believe that the solution for suffering is a hedonistic living for the moment only such as some modern interpreters of Buddhism seem to advocate. The solution lies in living each moment to its fullest but also bearing *a sense of responsibility* for the moment with the awareness of its priceless quality that can never be held and never be regained; for even at this level the workings of karma are relentlessly carried on. Each action of the present etches its mark upon the mind, which in turn brings about the suffering of joy of the future. In such a manner man creates his own heaven or hell.

Although Nāgārjuna did not specifically discuss the subject of Naraka or hell, his sixth century follower, Candrakīrti did so and made the Mādhyamika stance very clear. In his famous commentary on Nāgārjuna's *Mūlamadhyamakakārikās*, entitled the *Prasannapadā*, Candrakīrti clearly states that Naraka is a creation of the unreal upside-downness (*viparyāsa*) of ignorant man, or in other words, it is the product of man's false discrimination.[19] It is just as in the case of the man who falls asleep, dreams that he is suffering in hell and cries out in fright; so those who cling to their evil deeds imagine that they are suffering in hell. But in reality, the visions of heaven and hell are merely gossamer mirages resulting from false clinging.[20]

The conclusion that the ultimate difference between heaven and hell lies in the attitude of the viewer is the basis of Mādhyamika philosophy which in turn, laid the first foundation for Mahāyāna thought. This concept was further expanded by the Vijñānavāda school, which formed the second foundation for Mahāyāna Buddhism.

### C. *The Concept of Hell in Vijñānavāda Philosophy*

The founders of the Vijñānavāda school are generally regarded to have been Vasubandhu and his younger brother Asaṅga, who lived approximately during the fourth century A.D. As the title of the school suggests, the main emphasis was placed upon the role of consciousness (Skt. *Vijñāna*) in attaining Enlightenment. The alternate name is Yogācāra (practice of yoga), which illustrates the accompanying desire for practical application of the philosophy.

Although the Vijñānavāda school was purely idealistic, it represented a logical outgrowth of Mādhyamika philosophy since their aim was to create a source of affirmation that transcended the seeming Mādhyamika negation. The Mādhyamikas had successfully proven the unreal nature of all existents and as a result the problem had arisen regarding 'what' remained to become Enlightened and how Enlightenment was achieved. Also by this time certain factions of Mādhyamika adherents were indulging in the false view of clinging to the concept of *śūnyatā* itself, a position that could only be rectified by the development of a new middle way. The Vijñānavādins sought to accomplish both goals by means of proclaiming the existence of a fundamental consciousness (*Ālaya vijñāna*), possessed by sentient beings during their lifetimes. It is this consciousness that ignorant men consider to be their 'soul', 'ego' or '*ātman*' and its germ dates back to the teachings of Early Buddhism.[21] The attainment of Nirvana in the Vijñānavādin view now consists of 'the revolution of the *Ālaya vijñāna*' which is termed '*āśrayaparāvṛtti*' or '*ālayaparāvṛitti*,' meaning that the mind of ignorance is transformed into wisdom.[22] The following is an account of the method by which this conversion takes place:

Initially, the Vijñānavādins considered the basis for subject-object discrimination to be the human mind or consciousness, a factor that they believed could be proven in analyzing the method by which consciousness functions. For instance, when the individual perceives an object such as a pen in front of him, a relationship is established between the "I" or subjectivity and the object cognized. This particular type of relationship, in which the object is presented to the mind in a tangible form, can only occur when consciousness is aware and functioning. If the individual is asleep or unaware of the existence of the pen before him, it has no immediate significance to him. The pen in effect must become a content of consciousness in order to assume meaning for the individual. In this respect we can say that the cognized pen represents the appearance of the pen upon the human mind, or that one aspect of consciousness consists in appearing as an object.[23] This aspect is known as the *Ālaya vijñāna.*

Naturally, consciousness cannot assume the aspect of appearing as an object without also at the same time appearing as the perceiver of this object, or the subjectivity. Thus both subjectivity and the object represent related aspects of consciousness and when either does not exist, consciousness cannot exist. In such a manner, consciousness forms the basis upon which the world as we know it comes into existence in the form of the interdependent relationship between subjectivity and its objects.[24]

The subjective aspect of consciousness responsible for cognizing the manifestations of the objective world is divided into seven categories consisting of:

*1-5 Five Sense Consciousness (vijñāna)*
eye-consciousness
ear-consciousness
nose-consciousness
tongue-consciousness
tactile-consciousness
*6 Mental Functions (mano-vijñāna)*
*7 Notion of Ego-or the consciousness that acts*
*as a centralizing unit (kliṣṭamana)*

The objective aspect of consciousness, representing the manifestation of the mind in the form of the objective world, is the *Ālaya vijñāna* and generally termed the 'eighth consciousness'. Literally, *Ālaya vijñāna* means 'store consciousness' and in turn influences future data. Tainted with ignorance, the *Ālaya vijñāna* works interdependently with each of the seven other consciousnesses and in turn discolours them. For instance, the false impression that objects in the phenomenal world are real, solid substances causes the notion of ego to utilize such fancied objects in order to affirm its own existence and mistakenly believe that it is also an independent reality. In the same manner the five senses are falsely assumed to be separate entities and so on. The *Ālaya vijñāna* stores and creates the mental and physical attitude of the individual which in turn influences the reactions of the senses and mental functions leaving no sphere free from the distortion and discolouration of ignorance. This is the Vijñānavādin interpretation of the World of Ignorance or Realm of Pollution. The main characteristic of this World of Ignorance is that individuals by means of discriminative knowledge fully assume phenomena, which do not actually exist, to be true independent entities. In Sanskrit this is known as *parikalpita-lakṣaṇa* (Discriminative Fully Assumed characteristic). When these ignorant men cling to the objective world, they falsely believe that they are grasping solid substance. In reality these phenomena are merely manifestations of the individual's own mind and he can never be certain of the degree of distortion that he has projected. It is this very distortion that makes these objects appear to be lasting solid substances. In order to break his circle of clinging, man must realize that the so-called objective world is actually empty or hollow since exterior objects have no ability to make themselves known as they really are. Since human beings are totally dependent upon their own minds to cognize the phenomenal world, the so-called objectivity that man clings to is in its essence void. What he believes to be real or lasting is in effect merely his own mental projection. All objects are as transitory and changeable as man himself, hence clinging to them is a futile effort destined to lead to frustration.

The next question that arises is, if the mind alone manifests the exterior world and is the only medium through which the world is understood, then what is the nature of the human mind? Although the mind manifests the exterior world, it does not exist independently of this manifestation itself. Even though the Vijñānavādins claimed mind to be the basis for understanding human existence, they did not believe that the mind existed independently. The relationship was understood to be mutual and the dependence of the mind makes it also void or empty in essence. Once the individual is capable of comprehending all the implications involved with this mutual dependence of mind and world, he is able to attain Enlightenment. This is identical to Nāgārjuna's understanding of *śūnyatā*. In both cases, the difference in the individual before and after the realization of true reality is merely that the subjectivity and objectivity of clinging are transformed into nonclinging. In the case of the Vijñānavādins, this change is seen to take place within the mind but even here the essential nature of the mind does not change, there is merely a transformation of the mental attitude. Therefore, even after the realization of the true nature of the mind and the world, the functional process of cognition continues as before but the vicious circle of clinging no longer exists. This conversion of the human mind from the state of ignorance to an understanding of true reality is termed the attainment of wisdom (*prajñā*). It is also known as "the wisdom of nonduality" from which the "'wisdom to purify the world" spontaneously issues forth.[25] The contrast between the World of ignorance and World of Wisdom can be viewed in the following diagram:

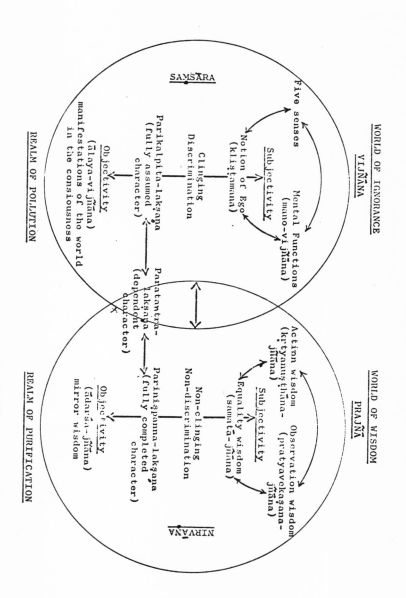

WORLD OF IGNORANCE
VIJÑĀNA

SAMSĀRA

Five senses

Mental Functions
(mano-vijñāna)

Notion of Ego
(kliṣṭamana)

Subjectivity

Clinging
Discrimination

Parikalpita-lakṣaṇa
(fully assumed
character)

Objectivity
(ālaya-vijñāna)
manifestations of the world
in the consiousness

REALM OF POLLUTION

Paratantra-
lakṣaṇa
(dependent
character)

WORLD OF WISDOM
PRAJÑĀ

Action wisdom    Observation wisdom
(kṛtyanuṣṭhāna-   (pratyavekṣaṇa-
jñāna)              jñāna)

Subjectivity

Equality wisdom
(samata-jñāna)

Non-clinging
Non-discrimination

Pariniṣpanna-lakṣaṇa
(fully completed
character)

Objectivity
(ādarśa-jñāna)
mirror wisdom

NIRVĀṆA

REALM OF PURIFICATION

65

Here we can see how the formerly tainted view of the objective world as manifested by the mind (*Ālaya vijñāna*) is transformed into "mirror-like wisdom" (*ādarśa-jñāna*). All forms of ignorance have been removed and the mind is now able to manifest the world with a mirror-like clarity reflecting it exactly at it is observed. No longer are egocentric desires projected upon the world nor do the senses, reflecting such an attitude, deceive the individual. This pure mirror-like reflection of the world-as-it-is forms the basis for the transformation of the other seven consciousness. For instance, the five sense-consciousnesses now are changed into "action-wisdom" which means that the senses can work to benefit others rather than merely serve the individual ego. Each of these becomes so purified that in effect, they are transformed into supernatural powers. At the same time the mental functions (*mano vijñāna*) have been converted into "observation wisdom." By this form of wisdom the data gathered from the senses are combined without any taint of illusion, and the Enlightened One is able to utilize this knowledge to teach and aid others. Lastly, the "notion of ego" (*kliṣtamana*) has been transformed into "equality wisdom," in which self and others are understood as interdependent oneness and this form of wisdom gives rise to the Enlightened One's compassion or positive actions on the behalf of others.

As the diagram implies, the World of Ignorance and World of Wisdom are not mutually different spheres. They represent the same phenomenal world as observed from a consciousness tainted by ignorance and a transformed purified consciousness. The realms are necessarily interdependent since Enlightenment can only be born out of ignorance. In each of these realm, existents assume specific characteristics which are assigned by the observing consciousness. Just as existents in the World of Ignorance took on the nature of the "Discriminative-Fully Assumed character" (*parikalpita-lakṣaṇa*), so the first step towards transformation is the recognition of the "Dependent Character" (*paratantra-lakṣaṇa*) of existents. Even common discriminative knowledge at times must recognize the dependent nature of objects resulting from the combination of causes and conditions. Occasionally the ordinary man is jolted out of his tendency to believe in the solid nature of exterior objects or even self and forced to admit that what he has believed to be eternal and unchangeable actually is not. This can happen when the physical body is stricken by illness or a cherished possession such as an automobile suddenly breaks down. Then the impermanence of the object becomes painfully apparent and the individual must admit what he had believed to be solid and lasting is as ephemeral as a mirage. This realization is a step closer to the World of Wisdom and can act as a springboard to Enlightenment since it is also a method of observing phenomena that are shared by the Enlightened Ones. Generally however, the Enlightened Ones' view of the existents can be classified as having a "Fully-completed Character" (*parinispanna-laksana*). This means that all existents are accepted as 'real' in the sense that 'reality' now assumes the nature of interdependent existence. This 'reality' is understood as changeable and transitory and through the wisdom of Enlightenment the comprehension is clear that no existent has a set form or permanent nature. Actually this third characteristic represents an ultimate affirmation of existence. The first characteristic (*parikalpita*) was a naïve affirmation of the reality of all existents and self as independent lasting entities. The second characteristic (*paratantra*) negated the first since ultimately every individual must recognize all existents to be dependent, subject to change and impermanence. But the final characteristic (*parinispanna*) once more affirms existence in a transcendental manner, asserting that all phenomena exist but in an indeterminate manner, interdependent and subject to change. Allegorically these three characteristics attributed to phenomena can be expressed in the following manner:[26]

On a dark night an ignorant man observes a coil of rope and mistakenly believes that it is a snake. He is so frightened that his hands and legs tremble with fear. The Enlightened One happening to perceive his error, attempts to educate the man to the reality of the situation but the ignorant man is so frightened and agitated that it is difficult for him to comprehend the instruction. Gradually however, he eliminates his ignorance and becomes aware that his imagined snake is merely a piece of rope; the illusion of snake is void (*śūnyatā*). This is the first level of his realization.

Still the man clings to the existence of the rope and believes it to be real. The next step entails the realization that the rope itself does not really exist. Its essence is hemp that has been created into a rope by various direct and indirect factors. It exists as a rope in merely the manner of a temporary mirage. In the future it will dissolve into strands or dust. Thus the rope can be said to be neither an existence nor a non-existence. The same can be said of the nature of the hemp which composes the rope, it also is neither an existence nor a non-existence. Thus the appearance of the snake, the rope and the hemp itself become separated and these symbolize the three characteristics attributed to existence depending upon the attitude of the viewer.

In the above allegory, the confused eyes of the ignorant man symbolize the "discriminative fully assumed characteristic" (*parikalpita*). The fears and trepidations the man experiences upon imagining the rope to be a snake represent birth and death, or the sufferings of human existence. The imagined appearance of the snake symbolizes the appearance of the false notion of self, and the awareness of the empty (*śūnyatā*) nature of the snake represents the awareness of the non-self (*anātman*) nature of man. The recognition of the rope represents the appearance of existents which are products of interrelated conditions such as tables, chairs, people, etc. The awareness of the *śūnyatā* nature of the rope symbolizes the awareness of the emptiness of all existents; while the temporary nature of the rope represents the "dependent characteristic" (*paratantra*). Realizing the fact that the rope actually does resemble a snake reflects the understanding of the temporary nature of the self. Finally, the hemp, which forms the essence of the rope, symbolizes the "fully completed characteristic" (*parinispanna*), representing the nature of ultimate reality.[27]

Upon viewing the foregoing diagram, it is possible to visualize how Vijñānavāda philosophy can be reduced to the view that the difference between the World of Ignorance and World of Wisdom simply lies within the mind of the viewer. The actual contents of both realms are identical since they merely represent the objects of daily life but the difference arises from the attitude towards them and oneself. If the desire exists to cling and possess, then the individual creates his own World of Pollution or hell in which his mind becomes his prison and his karma the chain that ceaselessly drags him onward to more suffering and torment. On the other hand, with the correct mental attitude, daily objects are transformed into the jeweled lakes, precious gem trees and golden pathways of paradise. The Vijñānavādins termed this transformation the conversion of *vijñāna* (consciousness) to *prajñā* (wisdom). Mahāyānists in general speak of it in terms of *"nirvāṇa* is *saṃsāra"* and *"saṃsārā* is *nirvāṇa"*; the so-called Pure Land schools of Mahāyāna Buddhism prefer to state that the Realm of Pollution (Hell) is identical to the Realm of Purification.

These concepts which are fundamental in Mahāyāna Buddhist philosophy are not limited to logical or rational comprehension. Indeed the asserted aim is to transcend discursive reasoning. A complete understanding is possible not only for the learned clergy but also for the laity who follow the path of devotional teachings. Such an intuitive understanding is the ultimate goal of lay teachings which commence with projecting heavens and hells into the future in order to induce the practice of virtue in the present. One of the clearest examples of Vijñānavāda philosophy realized in the life of a modern layman can be seen in the writings of Saichi Asahara (1850-1932) who was discovered by the late Dr. D. T. Suzuki.[28] Saichi was a Japanese geta maker, uneducated and nearly illiterate who had spent a long lifetime listening to the popular teachings of the Jōdo Shinshū sect. In his later years he began to avidly write down his impressions and feelings in a series of elementary school notebooks. In total he filled thirty-one notebooks as well as writing on assorted scraps of paper and even on the back of the geta he sold. The following represent his understanding of Mahāyāna philosophy:

I cannot fall into hell
Hell is right here.
This place is hell,
and hell is where we dwell.[29]

Where is Saichi's Pure Land?
Saichi's Pure Land is right here.
Where is the borderline of the Pure
Land in this world?
The eyes are the borderline of the Pure
Land in this world.[30]


Where is Saichi's Pure Land?
Saichi's Pure Land is in my heart.
It is, it is,
Namu Amida Butsu.[31]


This floating world is wretched,
but this floating world becomes the Pure Land.
I'm joyful
Namu Amida Butsu.[32]


In this world I enjoy the Pure Land
This world transforms into the Pure Land
I'm joyful
Namu Amida Butsu.[33]


Although Saichi had no formal knowledge of Mādhyamika nor Vijñānavāda philosophy, he was able to realize the essence of their teachings in his daily life merely as a result of the simple Buddhist instructions he had received. And he was also capable of realizing the fact that one who has been Enlightened does not permanently reside in the Realm of Purification but necessarily returns to the World of Ignorance.

A necessary feature of Enlightenment entails the return to the World of Ignorance in order to aid others to attain the same realization but this is not the only time when one who has been Enlightened enters into this realm. At times even he performs some of the same actions and feels some of the same human emotions as the ignorant man. As we earlier mentioned, even the historical Buddha spoke of the desire to increase his merit after he had attained Nirvana. This is because the Enlightened One, as a human being, still experiences human emotions but there is a difference in the quality of the reaction to these emotions. The same life experience that can create hell for one individual can lead another to the heaven of the Realm of Purification. As a human being, the individual who has attained Enlightenment is just as capable of mistaking a piece of rope for a snake on a dark night as the ignorant man. The difference is where the initial error leads the individual. The following diagram indicates the diverse directions that can be chosen and the snake in this instance can represent any life experience:

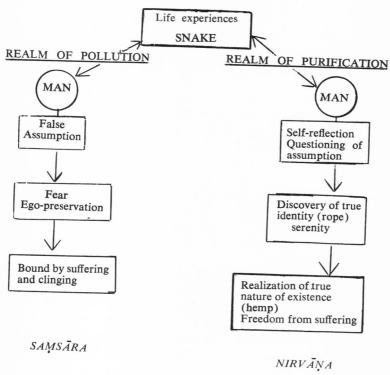

Hypothetically let us replace the snake in this diagram with the experience of facing the death of a beloved wife. The man who dwells in ignorance upon being confronted by such a tragedy will still cling to the false assumption that he and his loved one were immortal entities and in the face of such a shock is led to fear for his own ego-survival which has been placed in severe jeopardy by the loss of one who daily affirmed his own existence. These fears and the clinging to self lead him on to further grief and suffering. In contrast to such an attitude, the man who walks the path to Enlightenment will also suffer immediate grief upon losing his loved one; but he will reflect upon the nature of his grief and realize its basis lies in discrimination and clinging. Unconsciously he had supported the false assumption that this loved one would never leave him and he now becomes aware of that error. Once he engages in such self-reflection he immediately becomes conscious of the transitory dependent nature of human life and attains serenity in realizing that just as the leaves drop from the trees at the first frosts of the winter, so the natural law is for mortals to die. He also becomes aware of the fact that he has actually suffered no loss since neither 'he' nor his 'wife' were separate entities in the first place, nor has 'she' disappeared. The causes and conditions that temporarily formed her personality have dispersed but not ceased to exist; just as the flame of the candle appears and disappears. Upon the realization of this true nature of human existence, the man is Enlightened in the Realm of Purification and attains freedom from suffering. He has chosen the path to heaven rather than to hell. This is the essence of Vijñānavāda philosophy.

We thus complete our brief survey of the philosophical significance of the concept of hell. But philosophical theory divorced from actual practice has little meaning and is contrary to the spirit of Buddhism. The true impact of the Buddhist concept of hell can only be found within its power to stir or move the human mind towards change and transformation. To be successful, such a movement must be translated into concrete actions and this is the reason why eight symbolic Buddhist hells were created. Their purpose is to point towards the type of daily actions that are beneficial or detrimental to the attainment of ultimate freedom or Enlightenment. Of course, even in this area, the Buddhist hells merely point the way along the path and do not present a detailed guideline for every step of the journey. If they did, they would be depriving the individual of his own uniqueness and responsibility. Every man walks in a slightly different direction towards the goal depending upon the time, place and his own interior being which has been created by the effect of his past actions (karma). This is why of all religions, Buddhism is one of the most firm advocates of a variety of moral relativity. Unfortunately, such a stance frustrates those who seek to find a detailed road map to happiness. If such a map were available, then robots would be most assured of attaining the goal although incapable of appreciating it. One of the most important ingredients within man is believed in Buddhism to be his unique ability to create himself and in the process to mold his own heavens and hells. He also possesses the singular capability to rise above all that he creates and liberate himself, although he so seldom succeeds. These are the reasons why the path for each individual must be distinctively his own and no one else's.

Today, in a confused society, some modern intellectuals are turning toward what they believe to be Early Buddhism, believing it can offer the contemporary world a clear system of ethics to solve its ills. Unfortunately, the answers Early Buddhism presented were just as individualistic as later Mahāyāna since the guiding theme set by the historical Buddha was self-reliance.

The purpose of the Buddhist hells is to point to the way. It remains up to the individual to convert such signposts into personal daily actions. This is not always an easy task since the ego is perfectly capable of disguising itself as the conscience and using rationalizations to obtain its own ends. In order to penetrate through some of these illusions, we will now present the description of hell found in the *Sutra of the Remembrance of the True Law* with an analysis of its meaning. These will serve as more tangible signposts to fit the foregoing philosophical theories.

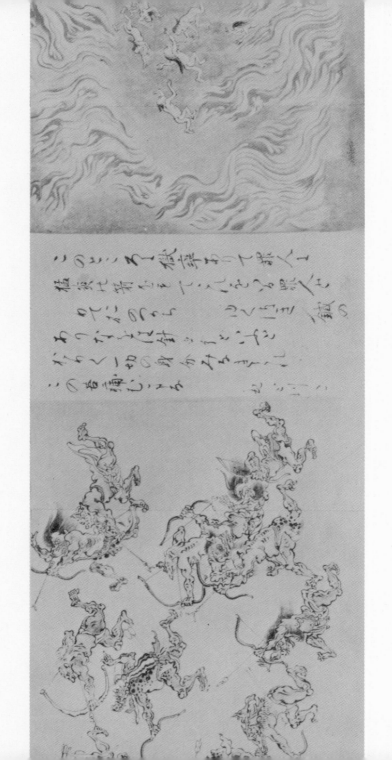

SECTION TWO


ANALYSIS AND INTERPRETATION OF THE
EIGHT BUDDHIST HELLS PRESENTED
BY THE SUTRA OF THE
REMEMBRANCE OF
THE TRUE LAW

# CHAPTER IV

# DESCRIPTION AND ANALYSIS OF THE EIGHT HELLS

## A. *The Text*

The *Saddharma smṛti-upasthāna* or *Sutra of the Remembrance of the True Law*, is generally believed to have been composed by Gautama Prajñāruci in India between the 4th and 5th century A.D.[1] The original Sanskrit text is no longer in existence and only the Tibetan and Chinese translation entitled *Chen-fa-nien-ch'u-ching* (Jap. *Shōbōnenjo-kyō*) which is found in the *Taishō Tripiṭaka* Vol. 17 pp. 1-379.

Although officially this work is classified in the Buddhist canon as being a Hīnayāna Abhidharma text, the context of the sutra reveals considerable Mahāyāna influence and the philosophical explanations closely resemble Mādhyamika and Vijñānavāda thought. The sutra failed to achieve prominence in India and received merely scanty recognition in China. Undoubtedly the official Hīnayāna classification deterred Mahāyāna scholars from displaying active interest in it, and despite the fact that this sutra contains the most systematized and lengthy treatment of the Five Existences, there is no evidence that anyone ever bothered to write a commentary on it. Only after the sutra arrived in Japan did it finally achieve a position of lasting fame by becoming a main source of Genshin's description of hell in his *Ōjōyōshū* (Essentials of Salvation), a treatise that made a deep imprint upon Japanese art, literature and popular religious sentiments of the time. It also served as a philosophical basis for the future development of Japanese Pure Land thought. Genshin however, greatly abbreviated the descriptions he selected from the *Sutra of the True Law* and the time has finally arrived for it to gain recognition in its own right.

## B. Background and Setting

The sutra opens as a group of newly ordained monks traveling in the vicinity of Rājagṛha are embarrassed to discover that they cannot answer the questions of a non-believer concerning the difference between the Dharma preached by the Buddha on morality and his own philosophy. Anxiously, the monks visit Śāriputra, the most learned disciple, to ask his advice but he directs them to the Buddha who is visiting Narada village at the time. Once they have finished explaining the nature of their dilemma to the Buddha, he preaches the teaching of the "Remembrance of the True Law" to the monks.

The sutra is exceptionally long and divided into the following sections:

*Chap. 1-2 Pathway of the Ten Karma of Goodness*
Summarizing the sufferings encountered in the hells by means of a discussion on the varieties of physical, vocal and mental karma in the belief that the recognition of improper actions will lead to their correction.

*Chap. 3-5 (first half) Discussion of Birth and Death*
Discussion of the philosophical nature of human suffering. The basic reason why individuals are bound by the circle of birth and death is because of their psychological desires that deceive them into falsely believing in the reality of their own independent existence and in the permanence of the

objects they covet. Only the Enlightened One is capable of realizing the emptiness of all things.

## Chap. 5 (second half) — 15 Discussion of the Eight Buddhist Hells

Their sufferings, immediate causes and subdivisions.

## Chap. 16-17 Preta Realm

Created by the greed and ignorance of man; destined for those who refuse *dāna* (offering) and are controlled by avarice. Dominant sufferings are hunger and thirst.

## Chap. 18-21 Animal Realm

A place reserved for those who have harmed animals, where they are tormented in a manner corresponding to the sufferings they have inflicted. The Asura, or fighting spirits, also reside in this realm and wage war against the heavenly deva.

## Chap. 22-63 Observations of Heaven

Consisting of the traditional heavens of the Four Deva Kings, Trāyastriṃśa and Yāma. This realm represents the human ideal of pleasure based upon ignorance. Above all it is transitory and subject to decay, which causes its inhabitants extreme suffering.

## Chap. 64-70 Remembrance of the Body

Explanation of the nature of the human body as subject to disease and illness. In particular, the impure, suffering, transitory and non-self *(anātman)* characteristics are discussed. This section also contains a group of mythological descriptions regarding remote lands and people.

Although only nine and a half chapters of the sutra specifically deal with the eight Buddhist hells, the entire sutra is devoted to the subject of hell in the broadest sense of the term. All Five Existences are depicted as realms of suffering and even the heavens bear their own unique torments. The cause for suffering is always the same — man deceives himself by following his desires and then proceeds to distort and struggle with reality. The existence of man is not dealt with independently in this presentation since the author obviously felt that the realm of man, symbolic of human reason, was inseparably related to the other four existences.

## C. Significance of the Hells

In the opening paragraph of the first hell and every major hell thereafter, the sutra repeats that the following view of hell represents the internal self-reflection of the devotee who follows the true Dharma and observes its practice. The hells are the dark labyrinths of the mind encumbered by the obstacles of ignorance and self-deceit. The purpose of this grotesque portrayal of human torment is to initiate the individual seeking Enlightenment into the horror chambers existing within himself where he can identify with the faceless anonymous sinners suffering immeasurable torments in the depths of the hells.

The essence of the discussion is the belief that the individual who reflects upon his own physical, vocal and mental actions in light of the true Buddhist Dharma, will be freed from the bonds of ignorance and attain Enlightenment. It thus represents a journey into self-reflection through the dim, corridors and pits of the mind that seeks to deceive itself. The constant theme is expressed as follows:

The painter of the karma of the evil mind
draws his retribution by means of his own karma.
Various different minds thus receive different sufferings.[2]

By means of self-reflection, the relentless circle of karma can be clearly understood and the individual is led to realize that there is no one to be deceived other than himself since he is the ultimate witness of his own actions:

> All sufferings are merely the result of one's own
> karma and represent its reward. The places of hell
> are painted by the brush of the painter's desire, within
> his mind. Improper discriminations are the various colours;
> wife and children are the paint containers and each individual
> is imprisoned by the cause and effect of his own clinging.[3]

Since the hells represent the creation of one's own mind as a result of egocentric desire and clinging; the purpose of self-reflection is to become aware of the existing mental condition. Even in this sutra it is obvious that such self-reflection assumes various levels and the presentations alternate between them. For the average layman of that day, self-reflection was believed to lead to an examination of moral conduct and serve as an incentive to practice virtue. Hell at such a level still remained a potential fate awaiting the wicked in the after-life. At the higher level however, self-reflection entailed the consideration of the doctrine of Inter-dependent Origination *(Pratītya samutpāda),* for it was believed to be ignorance of that doctrine that gave rise to the false belief in permanence and a lasting self, the cause of clinging. In Mahāyāna philosophy at this higher level, self-reflection turns to the entire problem of human existence in light of the subject-object relationship and here merely the realization that one had mentally created a psychological state of hell is sufficient to instantaneously transform it into the Realm of Purification. Of course intermediate levels can also be envisioned where individuals by means of recognition can extricate themselves from one or more psychological hells yet not develop adequate insight to gain total release.

From the viewpoint of the Enlightened Ones, the hells represent the realm where ordinary mortals pass their lives of endless clinging and grasping. Thus the hells symbolically predict the Enlightened One's view of the existing world from the "standpoint of the True Dharma" (lit. *Saddharma smṛti-upasthāna)*. In other words, the present world and actions of human beings are contrasted with an Enlightened world or Realm of Purification. From this stance, the upside-down posture *(viparyāsa)* of the sinners as they are symbolically described falling into the hells, represents the upside-down condition of the mind where truths and values are reversed. From this supreme level of reflection all the moral dictates of human society are viewed as being topsy-turvy, for social morality attributes far more weight to physical and vocal actions than to mental attitudes and the realm of appearances is valued far above the realm of insight. The following list of the eight hells and their causes clearly demonstrates the importance of psychological intention in the Buddhist world of self-reflection:

| Hells Caused by Physical Crimes | Causes |
|---|---|
| 1. Saṃjīva (Hell of Repetition) | killing |
| 2. Kāla-sūtra (Black-Rope Hell) | stealing |
| 3. Saṃghāta (Crowded Hell) | sexual indulgence |
| 4. Raurava (Screaming Hell) | intoxicants |

| Hells Caused by Vocal Crimes | |
|---|---|
| 5. Mahā-raurava (Great Screaming Hell) | lying |

| Hells Caused by Mental Crimes | |
|---|---|
| 6. Tapana (Hell of Burning Heat) | false views |
| 7. Pratapana (Hell of Great Burning Heat) | sexual defilement of religion |
| 8. Avīci (Hell of No-interval) | Five sins committed with premeditation |

## D.  Contents of the Eight Buddhist Hells

Ever since the period of Abhidharma Buddhism when the Buddhist hells were systematized, the number has remained constant with eight hot hells. *The Sutra of the Remembrance of the True Law* presents these eight major hells in accompaniment with sixteen subdivisions or minor hells for each, where specialized types of torments are inflicted in relation to specific actions. The following is a symbolic description of each of the major hells with an analysis of the moral causes for "falling" into the hell:

## 1) Saṃjīva (Hell of Repetition)

The first hell bearing the lightest retribution is caused by killing. Here those who take life deliberately and enjoy doing so are tormented with sufferings made to correspond to their actions. The three types of karma related to killing consist of: upper (the most severe), middle and lower. The upper variety belongs to the type of sinner who kills virtuous people or those who practice the Buddhist discipline, those who kill living things out of desire and those who destroy the source of life for other sentient beings. Once having committed such actions, these sinners experience no regret nor desire to repent. In fact they even praise their actions and encourage others to imitate them, such as the hunter who boasts of his trophies. When these people end their present life (psychological state), they are born into this hell. Depending upon the variety and quality of his karma, the sinner proceeds to be reborn in the various places of the hell corresponding to his past actions. Some only pass through one or two places before their karma is extinguished while others are forced to endure the suffering of all sixteen minor hells and still have remaining karma that will force them to stay in this hell for five hundred years calculated on the basis of time in the Heaven of the Four Deva Kings where symbolically one day and night is equivalent to fifty human years.

To give an example of some of the subdivisions of this hell, in the first minor hell, the Place of Excrement, those who have killed birds or deer without feeling of regret are tormented by being placed in a pit of hot bitter dung mixed with molten copper. The sinners stumbling through this filth are forced to eat it whereby the sharp beaked maggots inhabiting the dung enter into their bodies and consume their lips, teeth, tongue and everything in sight until the entire sinner is devoured. Thus those who have taken the lives of other creatures and consumed them are in turn devoured themselves.

In the fifth minor hell, the Place of Darkness, those who have slaughtered sheep by smothering them or killed turtles by crushing them between roof tiles suffer from a sinister dark fire that burns them while the fierce wind of the hell crumbles the surrounding solid diamond mountains into small bits and pieces that penetrate the air and tear the sinners' bodies. Although they attempt to scream out in pain, the sinners find that no sound comes forth just as the smothered sheep or crushed turtle formerly had no voice to cry out its agony. The pains of this minor hell are described by the sutra as representing the creation of the monkey of the human mind[4] which chooses to wander in the mountain of ignorance and roams over the peaks of illusion and pride; fickle and stupid it follows the paths of its own desires.

The type of killing deemed to be the cause of this major hell and all its subdivisions is an unfeeling, often spontaneous or emotional action. It is not the carefully premeditated type of murder that entails a realization of the seriousness of the crime, for such would be classified as a mental rather than physical action and confined to the eighth and final hell. Also, this is generally not the type of killing that is purely accidental for the sutra earlier clearly differentiates five light forms of karma that receive little or no retribution consisting of the following:

1) When a man walking unwittingly crushes an insect;
2) When an individual driving a stake into the ground or a nail into wood unintentionally destroys life;
3) When a doctor attempting to treat the sick involuntarily kills his patient;
4) When loving parents trying to correct their child by chance happen to kill him;
5) When a flame accidentally attracts an insect to its destruction.[5]

Such views obviously contrasted with those of the Jains and other groups of Indian philosophers who believed in the teaching of karma but adopted a far stricter interpretation of its results. The Buddhists interpreted this first hell as applying to those

82

who deliberately take life but at the same time are unaware of the value of life. This is the insensitive type of killing that is so clearly reflected in the attitude of the hunter. People of this nature are capable of destroying life as callously as the farmer reaps his grain.

No major distinction is made in this hell between those who destroy human life, such as the soldier on the battlefield, or mass murderer in society and those who take the lives of animals and insects. The soldier and hunter are deemed equally insensitive in appreciating the seriousness of their actions. This is the reason why killing in battle and killing for sport are both understood as physical actions requiring a minimum of mental deliberation. Buddhists would probably place abortion in the same category of crime and would find it difficult to comprehend why western contemporaries raise such stringent moral objections against the destruction of a human fetus yet show such little concern for the destruction of adults in war or even whole species of animal life. The reason why no distinction is made in Buddhism between the insensitive shedding of human blood and that of an animal or insect, is because of the belief that all living creatures have an equal right to survive. Man is believed to share the earth with other living things and is not given any superior right to perpetuate his own existence at the cost of other lives. Constantly the Buddhist texts refer to "sentient beings" rather than "human beings" to demonstrate concern for the universality of life. In view of such an attitude it is a foolish misinterpretation of the Buddhist injunction against killing to believe that the problem can be solved by becoming vegetarian. Even plants are considered to be living things possessing their own right of survival.

In Early Buddhism monks obtained their food by making begging rounds to the various villages and accepting whatever offerings of meat, fish or vegetables that were placed in their bowls. The Theravāda monks continue this tradition in modern times although it is not without its abuses, particularly in a highly civilized society. The Early Buddhists classified the types of meat which they considered to be "pure" and acceptable for the monks into three varieties:

1) Meat which a monk did not see killed for him,
2) Meat which he did not hear killed for him,
3) Meat which he knew without doubt was not killed for him.[6]

Such categories have little relevance in the modern supermarket and the literal observance of such restrictions today completely destroys the spirit in which they were originally written. The purpose was to discourage unnecessary killing but not to totally prohibit meat eating and even the historical Buddha is generally believed to have died as a result of pork poisoning.

For Buddhists the difference between meat eating and a vegetarian diet is merely a matter of degree rather that a question of taking life or sparing it. Some areas of popular sentiment even mistakenly believe that fish eating is less serious an offense than a diet of bloody meat but these are distorted views and abstinence from meat can only become virtuous when man realizes that he is incapable of surviving without appropriating some form of life to sustain his own. In this respect the Saṃjīva hell becomes unavoidable for all.

The essential point of this hell is to make the individual aware of his own human limitations and dependence upon other forms of life. Contrary to some world views, the Buddhists do not regard man as the conqueror of the universe but rather as one small dependent species incapable of existing without the aid of other life forms. They thus believe man must develop an attitude of gratitude and humility towards the plants and other living creatures that must be sacrificed for his survival and that he must not destroy these lives needlessly. This is the proper insight into the doctrine of interdependence and until man is capable of understanding his weakness and need for others, this hell remains unavoidable. It was the necessity for such humility that Shinran, founder of the Jōdo Shinshū sect, envisioned when he stated that 'if a good person could be born into the Realm of Purification, how much more so an evil man.'[7] What he meant was the fact that the man who can recognize his own human limitations and refuse to take pride in so-called virtuous actions is far closer to Enlightenment than those who believe in their own goodness.

Humility and the recognition of human weakness are key components on the path to Enlightenment. On the other hand, those who go to the opposite extreme and use the excuse of human frailty as a rationalization for avoiding personal responsibility deceive only themselves since man remains the ultimate witness of his own morality and there are no rationalizations to hide behind when facing the relentless consequences of one's own karma. The lesson of this hell is to take only what is necessary for life and to do this with a spirit of gratitude and humbleness. Gluttony becomes not only a sin against one's own body but also a needless waste of other lives. If the individual living in the affluent society merely restricts his intake to correspond to his actual needs, he will have no need for reducing diets or expensive machines to remove superfluous fat. The question in modern society becomes why does man need to prove his dominance by consuming everything that he sees? And the answer is that once again this is merely another manifestation of the desire to find permanence and stability in the face of ever changing reality.

## 2) The Kāla-sūtra (Black Rope Hell)

The official cause of this second major hell is stealing in conjunction with killing. The Chinese translation of *The Sutra of the Remembrance of the True Law* appears to be incomplete in this chapter and·it is most likely that sections were lost. For instance, three special places relating to the hell are described but these do not clearly represent any of the sixteen minor hells which are later mentioned by name but not described. There is also no clear explanation offered regarding the unusual name of the hell. Genshin in his *Ōjōyōshū* presents two traditional views drawn from other sources. According to the first, the demons of the hell catch the sinners and lay them on the burning ground.[8] They then mark their bodies with ink-blackened rope and proceed to slice along the markings with scorching iron saws or swords until the bodies are shredded into hundreds and thousands of pieces. In the second view, black iron ropes are stretched across the mountains of the hell with boiling cauldrons placed beneath them.[9] The demons of the hell force the sinners to carry heavy iron bundles on their backs and walk across the rope until eventually they topple and fall into the cauldron below where they are boiled. Most likely the author of the *Sutra of the Remembrance of the True Law* was familiar with the second version since in his description of the first place of special torment, he mentions ink-blackened ropes hanging from the mountains.

Among the three special places of this hell, the second or the Chandala hell, is reserved for those who use bedding, drugs or other objects destined for the sick, or take objects of which they are not worthy of using. In other words, sufferings here is destined for those who use objects they do not need or deserve as well as eating or drinking more than necessary. In this hell huge evil birds pluck out the sinner's eyes while the hell demons pull out his tongue and inner organs. The sinners are forced to drink molten copper liquid and be stabbed over all the surface of their bodies with three-pronged spears. The demons further vent their hatred by pounding and pulverizing the sinners and chase them with hot pokers and bows and arrows. Hopefully the sinners long to have their lives end but the constant torments are ceaseless until their karma is extinguished.

In describing this hell, the Buddha points out the fact that although individuals may commit their karma together or in groups, ultimately when the time for retribution arrives each individual is forced to suffer alone for his former actions. The only constant companion man has is his own karma and although relatives and friends all must eventually depart, karma follows the individual just as fragrance pursues the blossom.

The primary cause of the Black-rope hell and its subdivisions is stealing but it is quite obvious from the description of the Chandala hell that the Buddhist definition of stealing is not limited to a literal interpretation of taking that which does not belong to you. The implications are far broader and encompass the use of objects of which an individual is unworthy or undeserving. Just as in the case of killing, the purpose of this hell is to make the individual realize within the depths of his self-reflection his relationship of dependency upon others and the necessity for gratitude. Those who deprive other existents of life or property in the false belief

86

that as independent entities they are entitled to receive such goods or services are in reality stealing. Only the Arhat (lit. "one who is worthy or deserving") or an Enlightened One can rightfully receive from others since he alone is capable of comprehending the mutual relationship of all existents.

In the Buddhist view of worthiness, every living thing is believed to have a right to receive an equal share.[10] Such a standpoint reduces the rights of any single individual to a very minute degree. Furthermore, each individual possesses different abilities and capacities for work which may well make some more worthy of possessions than others. The ideal behind the Buddhist monastic life of renunciation was to arrive closer to the correct amount that each individual was deemed to be worthy of possessing, considering the equal rights of all. Despite such an ideal, it is impossible for any single individual to arrive at the exact amount in life due him and ultimately the difference between the monk and millionaire becomes merely a matter of degree. Every individual in some manner or another is guilty of stealing or taking more than he deserves since he constantly must sacrifice other forms of life to perpetuate his own survival. Although in some cases the degree of stealing is more advanced than others, all humans ultimately fall into this hell. It is only the attitude of non-clinging and comprehension of this mutual interdependency that can end such stealing and transform this hell into Enlightenment. For the laity, this hell was used as a means of setting forth the importance of gratitude as a virtue as well as teaching them to control their unlimited desires. Ultimately it sought to teach man the precariousness of his own existence and the need to drastically change his attitude towards life.

### 3) Saṃghāta (Crowded Hell)

The main cause for falling into this third major hell is killing and stealing combined with sexual indulgence. Literally *kāma mithyācārā* (Chin. *Hsieh-hsing*), (Jap. *Ja-gyō*) means "improper practice" but here it primarily relates to forms of sexual behaviour.

87

In the former hell the improper attitude towards possessions was regarded as stealing, and here in this hell, the improper attitude towards love becomes a sin. Before proceeding into detailed descriptions of the sixteen minor subdivisions of the hell, the problem of love in general is summed up in the sutra by relating one method of torture found in the hell:

The guardian demons of the hell lead sinners into a sword leaf forest with burning sharp leaves and as the individual sinner glances upwards, he suddenly sees a beautiful woman sitting in the top of the tree above him. Dressed in exquisite style and adorned by jewels, she appears to be a woman that he once knew and loved. Having seen her, his mind instantly begins to fill with desire and longingly he gazes at her silky hair, soft-oiled skin, slender long-nailed fingers and supple perfumed body. Every ignorant man in this hell who once gazes upon this woman is instantly drawn to her with the intense desire to possess her and inevitably he begins to climb up the tree to touch her. As he does so, the hot sword-leaves slice and hack his body, flesh, muscle and even shred his bones; but undauntedly, enduring the intense pain, he draws nearer to her. When he finally reaches the top of the tree, he suddenly discovers that she is now standing on the ground below him and looking up at him invitingly she calls out in tempting voice begging him to descend, saying; "Because of my desire for you, I came down here so please climb down and hold me." Immediately the sinner is again wracked by desire and begins to descend down the tree but at that instant, the sword-leaves reverse their direction. His body is torn and sliced once more and even his tongue and nose are cut open, while vultures swoop down and pluck out his eyes. Blindly and in great pain he reaches the ground and recovers but then he finds the woman is again appearing at the top of the tree. In such a manner the ignorant sinner passes hundreds of thousands of years vainly climbing up and down the sword-leaf tree.

The ironic part about this story is the fact that the sinner never becomes aware of his foolish repetition. Unlike the Greek hero Sisiphus, he can never transcend his ceaseless torture because he has no realization that it even exists. Every time that he sees the object of his desire, it appears to be different and this time more possible to obtain. As the sutra explains, "he is fooled by his own mind."[11] He never has the realization that his sufferings from the sword-leaves are connected with his futile attempt to obtain the woman he seeks. If he did understand this, he would be capable of ceasing his folly. This is identical to the situation of the ignorant man who creates his own hell, yet has no awareness of even being in a hell. He blames his sufferings upon countless outside forces or circumstances and never comprehends his own role of self-deception.

There is no question that the intention of this hell is to point out the tragedy of all so-called egocentric love and for this reason does not confine itself merely to sexual expressions. Time and time again it repeats the fact that the sinner is burnt by the fires of his own thirst:

> The fire of love is hotter than [real] fires, and
> in comparison all other fires are like ice.
> The fire of love fills the Three Worlds,
> and in comparison the fires of hell are as nothing.
> Love binds man and leads him to endless suffering;
> the fire of love is hell itself.
> Hell does not produce its own fire and
> the fires of hell can merely burn the physical body.
> The fire of hell is not omnipresent but
> The fire of love is everywhere and all the
> Three Worlds burn with such fire.[12]

"Love" in this sense denotes selfish desire or attachment and the comparison between the thirsts of desire and the fires of hell is repeated constantly throughout this major hell.

One variation of the theme occurs in the Fire-jar hell, or fifteenth minor subdivision. This is where self-proclaimed monks who reminisce about former experiences as laymen and forget to control their minds and remember the Dharma are punished along with those who greedily seize more than their share of food for the sick, medicines or bedding. This jar-like hell is filled with intense searing flames and the sinner contained inside it becomes like a flaming tree. Countless small fires burn on various parts of his body until finally they unite into one searing mass. As he opens his mouth to scream, the flames enter inside and scorch him. Rolling upon the ground in agony, the flames creep into his ears and other organs. In such a manner his flaming torments correspond with his former actions. For instance, his tongue is burnt for forgetting the discipline and indulging in food and drink while his eyes are burnt for clinging to the image of a beautiful woman. His ears and nose are scorched for listening to her laughter and inhaling her sweet perfume, until ultimately all his organs are consumed by flames. The conception of such a hell is clearly derived from the famous "Burning Sermon" of the historical Buddha, where he related how the five sense organs and their objects all burn with the flame of desire.[13] Such endless cravings bring constant torment and increasing desires for more satisfaction until eventually the individual is completely consumed. When those seeking Enlightenment consider how they constantly experience the thirst of love for humans as well as exterior objects in the daily human world, then they must realize in their self-reflection that this hell is an unavoidable place.

### 4)  Raurava (Screaming Hell)

The cause of this hell is the use of intoxicants combined with killing, stealing and sexual indulgence. Symbolically this is expressed by having the hell demons pry open the mouths of the sinners and pour in molten copper, allowing the boiling liquid to course through the entire body and burn all the interior organs.

Although it might be imagined that this hell relates merely to drinking liquor and is thus avoidable for many individuals, such is not the case. The hell does deal with the problem of over-indulgence and the demons recite how such individuals tumble into the hell laughing,[14] but the main emphasis is upon the improper *use* of intoxicants. The sixteen minor hells enumerate such causes as giving liquor to monks to confuse them, plying women with intoxicants for purposes of seduction, adding water to liquor to gain extra profits, giving animals alcohol to facilitate capture and plying individuals with drink in order to kill or rob them. From such descriptions it is obvious that the minor hells are not concerned with personal use but rather with improper usage.

During the lifetime of the historical Buddha, although there were injuctions against the use of liquor for the monks and one of the five observances (*śīla*) for the laity also mentioned drinking, there were certain occasions when the Buddha himself sanctioned its use.[15] Mahāyānists chose to follow the spirit of the discipline rather than a literal interpretation and considered that the main reason why the historical Buddha set forth a prohibition against liquor was due to the geographical and social environment of India.[16] The Theravāda tradition has maintained a strict abstinence from liquor although they do permit smoking, a habit that came into existence after the lifetime of the historical Buddha. The modern Mahāyāna attitude has only condemned the use of alcohol in a manner that hinders the practice of morality. From this standpoint it is believed that for some it is necessary to permanently abstain from liquor, while for others drinking in moderation is acceptable. The whole question of whether drinking should be allowed or not is believed to be decided upon the basis of each individual's condition, position and the time and place. One of the primary reasons for the development of such a liberal view in Japan was the result of the secularization of the clergy, primarily initiated by Shinran, founder of the Jōdo Shinshū sect.

Although the *Sutra of the Remembrance of the True Law* is officially a Hīnayāna text, it does not devote much time to the effects of the individual's personal use of intoxicants but rather deals with those who sell liquor for outrageous profits or use it for the purpose of manipulating others. No less than four minor hells are devoted to liquor dealers and the most interesting of these is the Hell of Complete Darkness where sinners are randomly ambushed in the dark by the demons and live in fearful terror. Such a suffering is quite appropriate for the business world where those who seek unreasonable profits must live in perpetual fear of losses. However, liquor dealers who water their stock are no more culpable than the butcher who adds false weight to his meat, the baker who inflates his bread or the stockholder who deceptively causes his shares to rise. All equally deceive the public and live in perpetual fear of being attacked in the night by a decline in prices or demand. This hell thus beckons to all who engage in business and seek lucrative profits since the Buddhist concept of a reasonable profit consists of merely enough to earn a sufficient livelihood.

We can also note that although this hell relates to drinking, not a single subdivision describes the individual who drinks and enjoys liquor by himself or in the company of friends. At the end of the description of the minor hells, the demons present a general discussion of the evils in drinking and point out that it destroys the organs, confuses the mind and makes man like a sheep not knowing what to do or not to do, and because of this they advise giving it up.[17] They also point out that those who become intoxicated are like dead men and that if a man does not desire to die, he should not drink. However, despite such warnings, the major motive of this hell is to lead profit-seekers and those who attempt to manipulate others for their own goals, along the path of self-reflection. Manipulation can be accomplished with drugs just as easily as alcohol but it can also arise from far less dangerous items such as gifts and promises; even intimidation ranks as a variety of manipulation. In this respect everyone is guilty since even those who do not use intoxicants or seek excess profits do use others to gain their desired goals.

### 5) Mahāraurava (Great Screaming Hell)

The prime cause of this hell is lying or improper words in conjunction with the crimes of the former hells and befittingly, most of the sufferings of this hell pertain to the tongue and mouth. Being the only hell caused by vocal actions, the causes of the subdivisions of this hell offer far more psychological insights than those of the previous hells.[18] It is also the first hell where the mental condition of the sinner is clearly related to the crime, and fear appears as one of the most frequent motives. For instance, in the minor Hell of Unbearable Pain, sinners who commit perjury or bribery suffer by having snakes born within their bodies. These snakes are symbolic of inner fears such as inadequacy, punishment, loss of cherished possessions and so on. Gnawing at their sinner's entrails, they cause endless torment and although outwardly such people might appear to be successful and happy, inwardly they live in agony. Each lie in turn creates further bondage and fear, in effect giving birth to a new nest of vipers.

In Mahāyāna thought lying can be observed in a broad connotation as representing the natural subjective differentiation between exterior phenomena which occurs in all forms of human discourse. This corresponds to Nāgārjuna's definition of *prapañca,* which at times has been defined as "false statements," or "fancy imaginings." As a distortion of reality, *prapañca* is identical to lying and the historical Buddha once stated:

> To each man born, an axe grows within his mouth,
> wherewith the fool who speaks improperly cuts himself.[19]

All human words represent this axe carving away segments of reality and allowing us to see only the distorted pieces. In daily life most individuals can easily recognize the obvious lies confronting them by advertising, in the news media, on television, or in political campaigns but few are capable of comprehending the fact that their whole lives are based upon lies. The difference once again becomes merely a question of degree. The majority of so-called truths that men struggle and die for are so often distortions created by their own egos or the collective ego of their society. In Buddhism, there can be no clear separation of truth and lie, black and white in the phenomenal world, but this does not mean that one should deliberately deceive others under the excuse that everything we see is some form of illusion. Such a weak excuse will not stop the relentless cycle of karmic retribution. It does mean that individuals should examine and question the so-called 'truths' they personally accept as well as those that society presents them. This hell becomes unavoidable for all since everyone is guilty in some form or another of false words and false understanding.

### 6) *Tapana (Hell of Burning Heat)*

The major cause of this hell is false views accompanied by the crimes of the former hells. Here, in this raging inferno, the sinners' bodies which are as tender as young grass, are consumed by roaring flames. In comparison to this intense heat, the former hells appear as cool as snow to the suffering sinners.

As the first hell related to mental actions, this naraka attacks what are considered to be the major hindrances to Enlightenment. Primary among the false views enumerated is the denial of the law of cause and effect (or karma), which would nullify the need for Buddhist morality. In the same vein the denial of the existence of good and evil is condemned. During his life-time, the historical Buddha attacked both such opinions as deterrents to the practice of personal responsibility.[20]

Another false view cited is the denial of *dāna*, which in its broadest implication covers spiritual as well as material giving in all phases of human life. A similar false view that would also contribute to social chaos is the belief in abolishing all forms of meetings ranging from the family to the national level. Such were evidently extreme opinions set forth by various radical contemporary Indian groups.

Besides these dominant varieties of false views, the subdivisions of the hell attack other contemporary practices considered to be superstitious or conducive to evading personal responsibility. For instance, in the Puṇḍarīka Minor Hell, those who mistakenly believe they can obtain birth in one of the deva heavens by practicing starvation and encouraging others to do likewise are tormented by the sight of a lotus pond and forest in the distance with cool water and singing birds. The demons of the hell urge the sinners to escape the hell fires by running to this peaceful oasis but as they enter the pathway, the sinners discover it is filled with burning charcoal and studded by firepits. After encountering numerous torments along the way, such as being blinded

94

by insects who devour their eyes, the sinners finally reach the lotus pond but fail to realize that it is merely another inferno with lotus-colored flames. Deceived by their karma, they believe they have indeed arrived at an oasis and climb upon the flaming lotuses to seek coolness and sit there until they are consumed by flames.

Misguided individuals who set fires in the forests, fields and along the beaches in hope of pleasing the fire god and attaining a deva heaven receive for their punishment birth into the Hell Where Everyone is Cooked. Here they suffer by seeing the vision of their wives, friends and beloved parents burnt in the flames. Although the loved ones call to the sinner for help, he has no means of aiding them and being forced to witness their pain, he suffers sixteen times greater than being burnt himself in the hell fires.

In contrast to those who perform extreme practices in the hope of future birth in a heaven, the minor hells also attack those who propagate various other types of false teachings to others. For instance in the Dark Fire Wind Hell, those who teach that the human body is impermanent but the four great elements are eternal, suffer by being blown up into the air by an evil wind that spins them until they become invisible and then smashes them into dust. Also in the last subdivision. The Diamond-Beak Hornet Hell, those who teach the universe had an origin are tormented by the demons who pull out their hair by the roots with thin pliers and stuff it into their mouths, forcing them to eat it. At the same time diamond-beaked hornets sting them and cause blood to spurt out. This the demons then force the sinners to drink and it is extremely bitter in taste. But the more the sinners eat and drink, the more hungry they become until deceived by their minds, they commence to chew upon their own flesh. Such are the punishments for those who espouse views that are believed to be hindrances to Enlightenment.

Although Buddhists traditionally have a reputation for great tolerance, the author of this sutra clearly condemns the attitudes considered to be erroneous from the time of the historical Buddha. Other philosophical stances besides those mentioned consist of believing the world and its inhabitants are the creation of Maheśvara (Molten Copper and Mini Fish Hell), those who teach that all existents came into being and disappear without cause, like a mirage (Diamond Bone Hell), those who believe that all virtue and evil is predestined (Black Rope and Pain of Release Hell) and those who teach that either nothing exists or else everything is eternal (Crocodile Hell). It is interesting to note that none of these condemnations are directed at other Buddhist sects. All are varieties of false views condemned during the lifetime of the historical Buddha. The major criteria for selecting these views were that in some manner or another they encouraged individuals to evade personal responsibility for their actions and thus undermined morality. In the case of the extreme ascetical practices, these were deemed to be methods of evading personal responsibility insofar as it is easier to temporarily torture the flesh and be assured of a happy rebirth than to live a full life of daily self control. Other methods deprived the individual of choice, such as the belief in predestination. Modern acceptance of deterministic astrology and fortune telling are ancient remnants of such practices condemned by the historical Buddha.[21] Following a prescribed course in life stifles human initiative and deprives man of his precious ability to observe the consequences of his own actions. It is far more noble to create one's own destiny, and suffer the consequences, than to timidly wait upon the moods of the stars and planets before acting.

The major reason why the causes of this first hell resulting from mental actions are so serious is because they make the possibility of Enlightenment remote for the individual. The key to Enlightenment lies within the human mind and if that mind deceives itself or creates its own obstacles, then hope diminishes. Besides the foregoing varieties of false views, the religious who is deluded by sins of pride, greed or ambition, believing them to be worthy goals can also fall into this hell, as well as those who are guilty of "false Enlightenment." These are particularly subtle dangers awaiting individuals who believe that they have transcended the morality set forth for the common laity. The Bone-eating Insect Hell offers an example of such delusion. Here those who have burnt their bodies with dry cow dung in order to be born in the Brahmā heaven suffer by having their own bodies grow so large that they fill the entire hell. After becoming such a veritable mountain of flesh, these sinners are burnt by tremendous fires as well as forced to endure other physical torments that they experience more acutely because of their immense size. This is fitting symbolism for those who wallow in the false pride of ascetical penances while actually seeking some form of tangible gain. Such a hell is a particular danger for the religious who is tempted to take pride in his good deeds and be led into the delusion of false views. Perhaps it can be said that 'if even the evil fall into hell, then how much easier it is for the good to arrive there.' The layman who commits obvious socially condemned physical or vocal sins can more easily become aware of his wrongdoing than the religious, who may be equally sinful in pride, greed or avarice and yet be respected by society. This is why these mental hells are so dangerously deceptive and the hope for escape from them is far dimmer than in the former hells.

## 7) *Pratapana (Hell of Great Burning Heat)*

The hell destined for those who sexually defile religion. It is described as having tenfold greater pain than the foregoing hells and is inhabited by fierce demons with huge black bellies, flaming eyes and hooked fangs. These creatures grab the sinners by the throat and deliver them to the hell after first dragging them hundreds of thousands of yojana over mountains, through cities and even across oceans.

The various causes of this hell primarily relate to the seduction of nuns, monks or virtuous laywomen and these are graphically described. In the Burning Hell of String-like Worms, sinners who tempt laywomen are made to suffer by being tied and laid down on the burning hell floor, studded with iron hooks. As they begin to cry out in agony, the demons then take a bowstring-shaped worm and insert it into the anal orifice. This worm with its sharp teeth, burning sensors, and poisonous sting scorches its entrance into the body and then proceeds to devour the sinner's entrails as it releases its painful poison. Gradually, it works its way upwards through the body, consuming whatever it touches until it arrives at the head. Here it makes its escape by cracking open a hole in the skull and slithering out.

In the Place of Painful Hair special torments are devised for the woman who tries to seduce a virtuous monk. She is described as being a well-born housewife who threatens the monk who visits her home that if he refuses to have relations with her that she will tell her husband and publicly announce that he has raped her. On the other hand, if he accedes to her wishes, then she will provide him with ample food and drink while proclaiming his holiness to all. Such a woman is punished in this hell by having her skin pared off by the demons with a sharp-bladed knife until merely bone remains and as new soft flesh grows in, the process is repeated. At other times the demons amuse themselves by only peeling off small sections of flesh and then roasting the exposed portion. As she runs to escape from such torment she beholds the monk that she formerly tempted approaching her. Rushing into his arms to embrace him, the moment she touches him, the vision transforms into searing flame. Thus she suffers until her karma is exhausted but this is not the end of her misery. It is almost as impossible for such a woman to become a human again as it is for 'a turtle floating on the vast ocean to happen to stick its head through the hole in a random piece of driftwood.'[22] But if she does arrive by chance at the human state, then she will be born as an ugly hag with no parents or relatives; will be handicapped by the loss of an eye or ear, have a hare lip and ugly complexion. During her lifetime she will be forced to spend her time cleaning excrement, know only subservience and be beaten even by children.[23]

Although the Pratapana hell tends to deal primarily with the division between the laity and members of the sangha, in a broader interpretation it can also deal with all individuals who damage the chances of another to attain Enlightenment by enticing them into sexual relationships, improper beliefs and so on. The sutra points out various fallacies propagated by individuals who seek to tempt others such as saying that it is possible to obtain merit (*puñña*) without practicing *dāna*, that without *dāna* one can obtain Nirvana, or that the Buddha and his disciples do not possess true wisdom and the Buddhist Dharma should not be practiced. By means of such temptations Buddhist nuns and virtuous women are led to fall from virtue.

In the contemporary world, if we consider all the different means by which individuals are encouraged to follow their desires and abandon the struggle for self-control, then we will have to conclude that the advertising media are most guilty. It is by this means that modern man receives the greatest temptation to desire objects which he not only does not need but that in many cases are harmful to him. Those who encourage others to lie or deceive, or even force them into improper social conformity are equally culpable. These actions all damage the chances of others to attain Enlightenment and thus become gravest crimes. In the end this hell is also virtually unavoidable since every individual at some time or another during his lifetime deliberately or through negligence, encourages others to perform actions that he knows ultimately will do them harm.

## 8) *Avīci (No-Interval) Hell*

The name of this eighth and final hell is derived from the manner in which it appears to the sinners as they drop downwards upside-down for 2,000 years before arriving at its depths. As they fall, they lament:

> Only the flame and nothing but flame.
> The sky is covered in every direction
> with flame without interval and the
> earth is covered: — On the ground
> evil sinners are crowded and there is no
> place for me to rest. I am lonely and without
> friend, existing in the darkness of
> evil enveloped by raging flame. Even
> falling down from the sky, I can see neither
> sun nor moon nor stars.[24]

Sufferings here are a thousand times more intense than those encountered in the previous seven hells and their subdivisions

99

and the sinners enviously look up towards the previous hell where sinners seem in comparison, happy as the inhabitants of the highest deva heaven. But if a deva were even to smell the odor of this hell, he would instantly perish and every sinner reeks of the foul stench. Even if it were possible for anyone to hear the sounds of the sufferings in this hell, that person would immediately die of terror.

The primary cause for arriving in this deepest hell is to commit one of the traditional Five sins of Buddhism (Pa. *pañca-anantarika-kammāni*), which have been condemned from earliest times.[25] These "crimes" or "forms of opposition" consist of:

1) Premeditated murder of one's natural mother
2) Premeditated murder of ones' natural father
3) Premeditated evil intention to harm the Enlightened One and rejoicing in such an action.
4) With premeditated evil intention to destroy the Buddhist community.
5) Premeditated murder of Arhats.

Repeatedly the sutra points out that these crimes must be committed with deliberate intention or premeditation and this is the reason why such acts of murder do not fall into the simple category of killing. Such crimes thoroughly contradict the basic good instincts of man and the person who takes life in this hell is fully aware of the nature of his action and its consequences.

Initially in Early Buddhism, the condemnation of such offenses was a natural by-product of social morality. These crimes represented the highest level of destruction of the foundations of society and the Buddhist community. But even in Early Buddhism the terms symbolically referred to those who acted totally contrary to Buddhist teachings. These people's minds were inverted and hardened and even at this period the upside-down position of the sinners as they fell into the hells symbolized their reverse views (*viparyāsa*). This hell more than any other emphasizes this upside-down posture of the sinners commencing as they enter the hell by falling for 2,000 years in such a position.

The inverted views of the individual are the cause of his hardened desire to destroy the opportunity of others to attain Enlightenment. This problem is particularly dealt with in the subdivisions of this hell where those who damage objects relating to the teachings are attacked. For instance, in the Hell of Rapid Pain, sinners who have destroyed the paintings or writings of the Buddha, making the Dharma-body disappear and thus deprive others of the opportunity to learn the true Dharma suffer in this place by having molten copper or hot sand poured into their eyes while their hands, guilty of destroying the Dharma, are sliced by the demons with sharp swords. Such actions against Buddhism or the Buddhist community are believed to deprive individuals of the opportunity to learn and possibly attain Enlightenment in the same manner as those who deprive others of life are destroying their chances for Enlightenment. In this manner we can view a progression in the mental hells from obstructing the possibility of one's own Enlightenment in the Tapana Hell, to damaging the chances of another for Enlightenment in the Pratapana, and now finally in this deepest hell, the complete destruction of another's chances for Enlightenment by either depriving him of his life or the opportunity to know Buddhism. Such actions are in total contradiction to the role of the bodhisattva, and although superficially it may appear that this hell is avoidable for many individuals, such is not the case.

The type of deliberate killing listed as one of the "Five forms of opposition" is extremely symbolic and extends far beyond a mere literal interpretation. According to the doctrine of Interdependent Origination (*Pratītya samutpāda*), all existents are mutually related as close as ties of blood kinship, which means that 'every female creature represents a natural mother, just as every male creature is a natural father.'[26] Such a relationship would make the individual who purchases a mousetrap or insecticide guilty of deliberate murder, although he may rationalize his actions under the guise of self-preservation. This does not mean that humans should passively surrender themselves to be overrun by rodents or so-called "pests", but it does mean that they should strip away the hypocrisy of self-deceit and admit their deliberate 'crimes' against other forms of life. This is the weakness that Shinran found every man to possess and hence be incapable of any 'good' actions. For instance, the monk who finishes his meditation may deliberately swat a fly on his forehead while feeling virtuous upon having completed his holy duty. Such a person creates his own hell of self-delusion and moves a step backwards from his professed goal. One of the earliest Buddhist texts, the *Dhammapada* states:

All tremble at punishment. All fear death; comparing others with oneself, one should neither kill nor cause to kill.[27]

To take another life, ultimately means to destroy a portion of oneself under the intricate workings of the Doctrine of Interdependent Origination.

The most serious of 'the Five Forms of Opposition' since the days of the historical Buddha has always been to injure the Buddhist community. Although in modern society persecution seldom exists, the insensitive use of Buddhist symbols and terms in such a manner as to denigrate the image of Buddhism falls into this category. Contemporary Buddhists have been hesitant to speak out against such abuses since they are aware images and symbols are merely guideposts *(upāya)* and should not become objects of attachment. Zen patriarchs even spoke of burning the statues and scriptures to counteract the tendency to grasp the means as a goal. On the other hand, the image or symbol represents one of the most important *upāya* to lead men to Enlightenment and to ridicule it or use it jestingly not only damages its use for other individuals but in turn injures the image of Buddhism itself in the eyes of the general public. In contemporary society damage to the 'public image' is far worse for the cause of Enlightenment than the physical destruction of temples or religious objects.

The injury of the Buddhist community is also a sin that can be felt by those who believe themselves to be Buddhists. Whether they have inhibited the functions of the Dharma-body by means of their pride, jealousy or bad example is a question that they must answer within the depths of their own self-reflection.

It is obvious upon observing these various eight hells that their aim is to present varying degrees of conventional morality. Literally, they can be accepted by the laity as future rewards in the next life resulting from improper actions during this lifetime. For the more spiritually advanced, the hells offer varying degrees of spiritual insight inducing self-reflection and serving as skillful means (upāya) to advance along the path to Nirvana. The author of the text however, was not content to merely confine his view of suffering to the actual hells but also wanted it to be clear to his readers that no goal was satisfactory short of Enlightenment, not even the highest heavens.

## E. Sufferings Encountered in the Highest Heavens

The portrayal of the happy heavens in the *Sutra of the Remembrance of the True Law* represents the ideal of Indian society at the time the sutra was composed. In other words, it reflects the perennial quest of people of all times for an ideal utopia fulfilling all human aspirations for comfort and convenience. Unfortunately, as this sutra demonstrates, the contentment of utopias is short-lived and man once again is plunged into hell, seeking to regain his lost paradise. The progress between heaven and hell is a perpetual form of reincarnation in human life. It was not by accident that the author decided to present life in the heavens to contrast with the sufferings of the hells, for this also demonstrates the futility of seeking any worldly form of lasting pleasure and contentment.

In accord with the Indian ideal, the residents of these heavens spend their lives feasting upon countless tempting varieties of food and drink while living beside a crystal lake covered with lotus blossoms and surrounded by a forest of mirrors reflecting their own physical beauty. They experience no difficulties, labor or obligations and every imaginable variety of human pleasure is satisfied. Wish trees exist to grant their immediate desires and when a heavenly denizen seeks to pluck a flower from one of these trees, the blossom blooms at his wish while the branch of the tree bends down to facilitate its picking. Even the color and fragrance of the flower will change in accordance with his desire, and if he but happens to think of music, the soft breeze of the forest will carry its melody to him. This is the idyllic life that the deva enjoy in their heavens until eventually, as individual karma (life) runs out, the joys turn bitter and there is no escape from decline. The male inhabitants of the heavens undergo five types of decay during their waning days in the heaven and each of these causes them immense suffering:

1) the body becomes weak and experiences cold sweat
2) the shining skin color fades and becomes dull
3) the five senses responding to various types of joy cease to function properly and hence no further joy can be experienced.
4) Because of his obvious physical decay, the individual begins to have a feeling of shame before other residents of the heaven.
5) The heavenly deva women with whom he once shared pleasure, now turn against him.[28]

The women inhabitants of these heavens undergo even greater psychological torments in their process of decay, perhaps because they cherish physical beauty more highly. As they decline, they undergo nine different sufferings:

1) The skin becomes loose, leathery and wrinkly.
2) The body does not balance well and becomes shaky. Because of this, the flowers that once bloomed over her head wither and drop.
3) Scarlet flowers that once bloomed beside her now fade into yellow.
4) When the wind blows, the heavenly soft seamless robe she wears turns into coarse, rough hemp.
5) When she attempts to fly in the heavenly air or walk on the ground, she now experiences tremendous exhaustion and the ground that used to spring at her touch seems to drag her back.
6) Her once pure and fragrant perspiration now is polluted.
7) As she reaches out her arm to pick a flower or fruit, the

tree branch now raises higher to avoid her and it is impossible for her to pick anything.

8) Lovemaking becomes ugly and tasteless.

9) When the wind blows her once soft hair, it now becomes coarse and dry.[29]

Each of these sufferings is related to the desires and as the decay of the body progresses, the desires of the mind increase to become ceaseless. More than ever before love-making is sought after, and the decaying residents pause even more frequently beside the crystal lakes and rivers to gaze at their images until they can no longer bear the sight. In the end, everything that had once brought them joy and happiness now becomes a source of torment and the heaven becomes a veritable hell.

## Conclusion

The Buddhist concept of hell is not a soporific to lull the masses into social conformity; for although such an aim might be desirable, it is not the goal of Buddhism. The aim is for the individual to attain Enlightenment and in this setting, hell represents the deceits and ego-coloured rationalizations that serve as hindrances to Enlightenment. The purpose of the eight Buddhist hells as presented in the *Sutra of the Remembrance of the True Law* is to induce self-reflection at the highest level, enabling the individual to break through the pitfalls of self-deception. At the lower level, they were intended to serve as means of instilling morality, but this was meant to be a first step along the path of religious awareness and not the final goal.

Every sect of Buddhism posits the same goal — Enlightenment — the difference between the various schools is simply a matter of individual suitability. For some meditation or esoteric ceremonies are more effective means, while for others the simple concentration upon the recitation of a Buddha's name is equally as effective. The concept of the Buddhist hells serves as such a means *(upāya)* pointing the way to Enlightenment and the purpose of the hells is to transform the nature of the human mind.

The key to Enlightenment has always existed within the human mind or attitude of observing life. The quality of the exterior world does not transform from hell to Enlightenment; the change merely occurs within the mind observing the world. To make this 'conversion' possible, the individual must suffer a jolt or shock forcing him to drastically change his views and ultimately his goals in life. One way of accomplishing such a transformation is by means of self-reflection and this is the aim in presenting the sight of the hells. All that is necessary is for the individual to realize that he is living in a hell or world of delusion for its quality to instantly change. The purpose is to gain a new perspective in life whereby the Interdependent nature of all existents is comprehended. Once wealth, material belongings or even loved ones are seen in proper perspective, ego-centered clinging can be vanquished. This does not mean that the individual should seek to escape life or destroy human emotions; but merely to acquire a new perspective free of self-colouration. To learn how to love without seeking one's own reflection in the loved one, to appreciate the good things of life without clinging to them and suffering in the course of inevitable change. It also means to realize one's ultimate freedom in the face of the shackling nature of modern society.

Constantly the purpose of the hells is to remind the individual that man is the ultimate witness of his own morality. He may successfully deceive the rest of the world around him, but ultimately under the law of karmic retribution, he will receive the effects of his own actions. On a larger scale the supra-self of society functions just as the individual under the law of Interdependent Origination and the actions of each of its members have a far greater effect than can be imagined. The hells serve as mirrors, exposing actions in their true light stripped of all rationalizations and deceit. Although an individual may offer a facade to the world of holiness, success or beauty, in the light of his own self-reflection he cannot disguise the stinking morass that truly exists. This is hell, and it is present everywhere like a constant shadow dogging each individual until it is recognized — and then it disappears.

# APPENDIX

Summary of the causes and torments found in the minor hells of the *Sutra of the Remembrance of the True Law*:

*A. Saṃjīva (Hell of Repetition)*
Major cause: Killing
Minor Hells:

### 1. *Place of Excrement*

Those who kill birds or deer without feeling regret are tormented here. Dung with a very bitter taste is heated and molten copper added. Worms with sharp beaks as hard as diamonds dwell within this filth. When the sinners stumble through it, they are forced to eat it whereby allowing the worms to enter into their bodies. Proceeding to consume the lips, tongue and teeth of the sinner, the worms move down the body devouring everything in sight until they finally have eaten the entire sinner.

### 2. *The Sword Circle*

Men who take the lives of other creatures by the sword are scorched in this flaming hell that makes the fire of the human world appear as cool as snowflakes. When the flame touches a sinner's body for even an instant, it explodes into thousands of small grains the size of poppy seeds. The name of the hell is derived from still another torment, a forest of sharp twin-bladed swords. The sinners are enticed here believing that it is a peaceful respite from the fiery hell and a place where they can quench their thirst. As they rush into the seemingly cool forest, the swords suddenly shower down and tear and slice their bodies into shreds.

### 3. *Place of the Cooking Pot*

Sinners who kill camels, boar, sheep, various birds, horses, rabbits, and bear, in order to remove the skin from these animals, cook, broil or boil them alive, suffer their retribution here. They are placed in a hot iron pot and boiled just like beans bubbling up and down in the frothy waters.

### 4. *Hell of Many Pains*

Reserved for those who torment or torture others. Those who crush, burn, smoke or hang other beings by various methods, who torment children or enemies are tortured in this hell exactly as they caused others to suffer.

### 5. *Place of Darkness*

Those who slaughter sheep by smothering them or kill turtles by smashing them between tiles suffer here from a sinister dark fire that burns them while fierce winds crumble the surrounding solid diamond mountains into small bits and pieces that pierce the air and tear the sinners' bodies. Although they attempt to scream out in agony they find that their voices will not come forth, just as the smothered sheep or crushed turtle had no voice to cry out its agony. The darkness burns on consuming them. The pains of this hell are described as being the creation of the monkey of the human mind which chooses to wander into the mountain of ignorance and roams over the peaks of illusion and pride; fickle and stupid it follows the path of its own desires.

### 6. *Place of No-Joy*

Those who kill or torment creatures by means of fearful sounds such as drums, the conch shell and shouting are afflicted here by hearing the terrible cries of evil birds and other creatures while their ears are devoured by sharp-beaked insects. As they voice their misery the Buddha compares them to the devil fish who floats in the stream of anger and resides in the mountain of birth and death. This fish, representing the ignorant mind, constantly desires sensual pleasures and upon obtaining such happiness smiles with joy. But when it must suffer in retribution for its actions, then it cries out in pain.

### 7. *Place of Extreme Suffering*

Individuals who have killed sentient beings because of hatred receive their reward in this hell of continual pain. When they are not being burnt by the searing flames, they are cast off high cliffs into the abyss. The constant pain reflects the endless burning of hatred within their own minds.

The other nine subdivisions are not described in the Chinese translation of the sutra although their names are listed and these present us with some notion of the types of torment they might inflict:

8) Hell of Diseases
9) Iron-paired Hell
10) Evil Stick Hell
11) Black Weasel Hell
12) Spinning Hell
13) Hell of Complete Pain
14) Padma (Red Lotus) Hell
15) Pond Hell
16) Hell of Torments Received in the Air

### B. *Kāla-sūtra (Black Rope Hell)*

Major cause: Stealing
Three special places:

### 1. *Equal-screaming Hell*

The description of this minor hell is very unclear and appears to represent an addition made by a later editor, perhaps to compensate for the missing sections of this hell. Those who deny belief in true morality and preach lies are punished in this place along with those who stealthily take other men's property and women. Here the sinners are hoisted up to high cliffs then prodded by sharp swords until they fall to the searing ground below; there they are devoured by iron fanged beasts. Even though they scream out their anguish, no one is present to hear or comfort them and they are forced to suffer alone. The demons taunt the sinners forcing them to remember that they are being roasted in this hell because of their own evil deeds committed while they were deceived by minds of hatred. If they could only control their minds, they would never feel any pain but now they must suffer for their actions and wives, children and relatives are all helpless to aid them.

## 2. *Chandala Hell*

Reserved for those who use bedding, drugs and other objects destined for the sick, or take objects which they are not worthy of using. In other words, suffering here is destined for those who use objects they do not need or deserve as well as eating or drinking more than necessary. In this hell huge evil birds pluck out the sinner's eyes while the hell demons pull out the tongue and inner organs. The sinners are forced to drink molten copper and be stabbed over all the surface of their bodies with three-pronged spears. The demons vent their hatred by pounding and pulverizing the sinners but there is no one to listen to their cries for help.

## 3. *Fearful Vulture Hell*

Awaits those who torment others in order to obtain their property or possessions. In this place the demons continually beat the sinners, chase them with arrows and hot pokers. Hopefully the sinners wish their lives might end but the constant torments go on ceaselessly. The Buddha in describing this hell points out that although individuals may commit their karma together in groups, ultimately when the time for retribution arrives, each must suffer alone for his former actions. Only karma is man's constant companion and while relatives and friends eventually depart, karma follows the individual just as the fragrance constantly accompanies the blossom.

The sixteen subdivisions are not listed.

## C. *Saṃghāta (Crowded Hell)*

Major cause: Sexual indulgence:
Minor Hells:

### 1. *Place of Reception of Great Pain*

Here those who commit improper sexual acts are burnt, stabbed throughout the body, cooked and boiled.

### 2. *Shredding Place*

Those who indulge in oral sexual practices have nails driven through their mouths and out the back of their heads by the hell demons. They also have bowls of molten copper poured down their throats and it penetrates scorching through their entire bodies until finally it escapes through the anal orifice.

### 3. *Hell Where Veins Are Cut*

Those who force women to have sexual relations are tortured here by molten copper as in the former hell.

### 4. *Hell of Evil Sights*

Here those who kidnap and molest children have the vision of their own children being physically tormented by steel hooks and pokers. They also are held upside down by the demons while molten liquid is poured into their anal orifices searing through their bodies until it burns out of their skulls.

### 5. *Gathering Hell*

Those who have sexual relations with cows or horses are tormented in this hell by seeing such animals. As they attempt to approach them with lust, the animals' sexual organs burst into flame burning the sinners.

### 6. *Hell of Many Pains*

Those who commit homosexual acts are attracted in this hell to a man of flame who burns them within his embrace.

### 7. *Hell of Enduring Pain*

Here those who have raped native women or passed them on to others while serving duty as victorious soldiers in a foreign country are hung upside-down from trees and burnt. As the flames reach their mouths they attempt to cry out in agony but instead of making a sound, the flame rushes inside their bodies to burn their innards.

### 8. *Chu-Chu Chu-chu Hell*

Those who live in areas where there are no women and have sexual relations with sheep or camels while despising the Enlightened One's, suffer here. Iron insects perpetually attack them biting their flesh, sucking their blood and eventually devouring their inner organs.

### 9. *"Why, Why" Hell*

Barbarians in periphery lands who commit incest with their older and younger sisters are born here and suffer from fire and evil birds. Also they are tempted by the sight of cool lotus blossoms appearing on the mountainsides. When they rush to these pleasant places demons attack them by dropping swords on their heads and birds pull out their organs.

### 10. *Hell of Burning Tears*

The person who forces a nun, who has previously broken the discipline and had relations with another man, to now have relations with him is tortured here. The great flames of this hell are so intense that even the sinner's tears of agony turn into flame and scorch his face and body.

### 11. *Hell Where All the Organs Are Destroyed*

Those who engage in improper oral and anal sexual relations

with the opposite sex receive their retribution in this hell. The torment is to have molten copper juice poured into their mouths.

## 12. Hell of No Other Shore

Men filled with lust who think of their own wives while having relations with other women suffer here by being cut by swords, burnt by hot ashes and afflicted with diseases. They have no hope of ever reaching the other shore (deliverance) and there is no one to comfort them.

## 13. Padma (Red Lotus) Hell

The monk who fondly remembers his sexual experiences while still a layman is sent to this hell. Here, while suffering in the midst of the reddish hued hell fires, he sees a cool lotus pond in the distance filled with red lotuses. As he rushes to reach this place he must run over a steel spiked road as he is chased by hell demons. Finally, when at last he arrives at the pond and climbs upon a lotus, it bursts into intense blistering flame.

## 14. Mahāpadma Hell

Those who claim to be monks and practice virtue in order to obtain the favors of heavenly maidens rather than attain Nirvana are born here. This hell has a molten copper river as well as deceiving lotus ponds as in the former hell.

## 15. Fire-jar Hell

Those who claim to be monks yet recall the enjoyments they had as laymen and delight in being near women suffer here. Every inch of this jarlike hell is filled with flame.

## 16. Hell of Fiery Iron Powder

Those who claim to be monks yet have strong desires while being near women and listening to their sounds are punished here. The hell is square and made of iron with constantly burning walls. Rains of fiery iron powder shower down on the sinners from above.

## D.  Raurava  (Screaming Hell)

Major cause: Intoxicants
Minor  Hells:

### 1.  Great Howling Hell

Reserved for those who give liquor to individuals practicing the Buddhist śīla and living a holy life. Here the demons of the hell dip molten copper from an iron bowl and pour it into the sinners' mouths. The pain is so intense that their howling fills the entire sky and incites the naturally fierce demons to become twice as angry with them.

### 2.  Hell Filled With Voices

The man who personally enjoys drinking and forces a young monk who has just received the śīla to drink, is destined for this hell. The sinners are pounded with an iron pestle and the sound of their screams fills the entire hell causing everything to disappear in its wake.

### 3.  Burning Hair Hell

Those who praise the virtues of liquor and tempt the faithful Buddhist layman to drink are tortured here. The sinner's entire body from his hair to his feet perpetually burns while iron tigers chew on his legs and flaming beaked vultures crack open his skull and pulls out his brains.

### 4.  Fire-insect Hell

Liquor dealers who add water to their merchandise to gain profit and thus steal from their clients are tormented by 404 diseases in this hell. There are 101 wind diseases, 101 yellow diseases, 101 cold diseases and 101 other various maladies. If the inhabitants of the four continents were exposed to even one of these diseases they would all die within the period of one night.

### 5.  Burning Steel Pestle Hell

Men who give liquor to wild animals in order to facilitate their capture are tortured here by a steel pestle that pounds them into dust. As they scream and try to escape from the hell the giant pestle chases them and continues to smash them.

## 6. *Twin Flame of Burning Stones*

The type of individual who makes an elephant drunk in order to have it rampage and kill others suffers here from a giant elephant who tosses him in the air and stomps his body to pieces.

## 7. *Slaughtering Hell*

The man who plies a good woman with liquor and has sexual relations with her is tortured here by having his genitals pulled out by a burning iron hook. As soon as they are removed tender new organs grow in again that are promptly pulled out. Eventually the sinners escape and run until they reach a great precipice. At that point they are confronted by horrible birds with steel beaks and claws. In terror to flee they fall over the cliff and the birds catch them in the air and devour them.

## 8. *Field of Steel Trees*

Individuals who mix poison with liquor and give it to their enemies here are tied to burning iron wheels. The demons of the hell then shoot arrows at them until not a single spot on their body remains untouched. When this torment ends, they are eaten by iron snakes.

## 9. *Hell of Complete Darkness*

Dealers of liquor who overcharge an unknowing buyer in this dark hell are ambushed by the demons who indiscriminately reach out to grab and strike them.

## 10. *Field of Yama-rāja*

Those who give liquor to the sick or a new mother in order to obtain their money, food or clothing are burnt in this hell, from the soles of their feet to their heads. The demons also chase the sinners and slash at them with flaming swords.

### 11. *Sword Forest*

Dealers who deceive travelers by selling them cheap inferior liquor while assuring them it is superior quality and will not make them drunk, causing the traveler to become intoxicated and to lose his life or property, suffers in this hell. Burning stones rain down from the sky tearing and slashing the sinner's body until they fall to the ground and vomit forth their tongues. There is also a river of boiling blood mixed with copper and platinum, the very sight of which frightens the sinners.

### 12. *Large Sword Forest*

Those who sell liquor along the road in a remote place to make exorbitant profit are tormented here by the sword-leaves of this forest. There is also a poisonous smoke that belches forth from the ground. Even one yojana prior to entering the forest the sinners' bodies begin to decompose and once they enter within the forest they are kept there by the demons who guard the entrance. There is no escape from the continual rain of sword-blades.

### 13. *Plantain Smoke Forest*

The man who plies a good woman with liquor in hopes of seducing her suffers in this smoke hell, that is completely filled with flame but totally darkened by the thick smoke.

### 14. *Forest of Burning Smoke*

Those who give liquor to enemies or government officials out of hatred and desire to see them suffer are tormented in this hell by winds as burning and penetrating as swords or fire. These winds sweep the sinners up into the air and then smash them into pieces no larger than grains of sand.

### 15. *Burning Cloud mist Hell*

Men who give liquor to Buddhists maintaining the śīla or non-Buddhists in order to shame them and laugh at them are forced by the demons of this hell to walk on thick fiery ground

116

until they melt. Then they are lifted up to return to life and commence their torture anew. There are also fire winds that blow the sinners into the sky like leaves and they are tossed and twisted about like tangled ropes.

## 16. *Differentiation of Pain Hell*

Men who give liquor to their slaves or workers with the idea that it will increase their physical strength or make them run faster and kill better on the hunts are tormented here. The demons of the hell follow the sinners and then select them here and there at random for various types of terrible sufferings.

## E. *Mahāraurava (Great Screaming Hell)*

Major cause: Lying
Minor Hells:

### 1. *Roaring Hell*

Destined for those who lie while quarreling with their friends and later feel no regret. In this hell the sinner's tongue grows to a length of three krośa and the demons of the hell spade a deep ditch through the middle of it and fill it with molten copper. Also worms are born on the tongue that eat it.

### 2. *Hell of An Infinite Number of Pains*

The man who untruthfully assures another that he has influence over his enemy and can cause him to act in any manner that he pleases, is tormented in this hell from all the pains of the first major hell as well as countless other forms of suffering that the text states are almost impossible to describe.

### 3. *Hell of Unbearable Pain*

Those who attempt to bribe officials or commit perjury for

their own benefit suffer in this hell from having snakes born within their bodies.

### 4. *Hell of Hatred*

Men who steal agricultural land from others by telling lies or using various forms of sophistry are tormented here by the demons of the hell who place them in fire and heat it with iron bellows. They are then plucked from the fire and pounded upon an iron anvil. After being heated once again, they are placed in water to harden.

### 5. *Hell of Total Darkness*

Reserved for the man who rapes a woman and later in public or before the king denies his action and causes the woman to receive punishment. In this hell the sinner's skull is cracked open and his tongue is pulled out and sliced to pieces by a sword.

### 6. *Dark Smoke Hell*

Destined for the man who has vowed with his friend to share all his wealth but later when he has made a fortune in a distant place, denies having made any profit. Here every part of the sinner's body is sliced open and later soft new skin covers the wounds but this is once again cut open by the ceaseless sword.

### 7. *Hell Where Sinners Fall Like Flying Insects*

The man who has obtained goods from the sangha, such as grain and clothing at a reduced price and then makes an exorbitant profit while lying to the monks, suffers in this hell. An iron tiger bites off his stomach and eats it while demons with flaming axes chop off other parts of his flesh and bone to feed to the tigers. A hot burning hook pierces his chin and his tongue is dragged out with burning tongs.

118

## 8. *Hell of Death and Rebirth*

Those who deceptively pretend to be monks in order to encourage innocent travelers to enter into the bandits' lair suffer here. Upon seeing a blue lotus grove in the distance, the sinners rush to reach it only to discover that the blue lotus light is actually nothing but flames. The demons then place the sinners among the fiery lotuses where parts of their body commence to drop off and as their legs fall off, they can no longer run nor attempt to escape.

## 9. *Rolling Hell*

Those members of society who are highly respected and trusted yet find occasion to lie and betray their trust suffer in this hell. In the distance the sinners can visualize their parents, children or friends attempting to comfort them and they rush towards them in hope of rescue but on the way fall into a great river where they are burnt and suffer. Having overcome this obstacle they rush on again but this time are forced to run upon a road filled with iron hooks while they are chased by the demons. Although they endure countless tortures they never arrive at their goal.

## 10. *Hell of Vain Desires*

Individuals who lie to the sick and needy and refuse to aid them suffer here from the vision of a cool refreshing forest in the distance. Feeling hunger and thirst they rush towards the forest but upon arriving there discover merely a pit of molten iron bearing a terrible stench that even scorches their noses. Eventually they fall into this fiery mass and burn and glow like fireflies.

## 11. *Twin Suffering Hell*

Destined for those who perjure themselves in a village or social gathering in hopes of punishing or destroying another person. In this hell, lions with flaming fangs pounce upon the sinners and gnaw upon them until they die. But once the lion drops their remains upon the ground they are revived to life once again and attacked anew by the beasts.

### 12. *Alternate Suffering Hell*

Those who lie, trick or conspire in order to gain an inheritance suffer in this hell. The sinner sees the relatives that he earlier deceived holding giant scissors and they commence to cut off his flesh and stuff it in his mouth forcing him to eat it.

### 13. *Hell of Diamond Beaked Birds*

The member of the Buddhist sangha who, after agreeing to care for the sick, later breaks his promise, suffers in this hell from a giant crow that pecks off pieces of his flesh. These promptly grow back again soft and tender and then are plucked off once more by the crow.

### 14. *Flaming Hair Hell*

Reserved for those who commit actions contrary to law or ritual at festivals. Later, despite the fact that their mistakes were witnessed, deny wrongdoing in fear of punishment. Here the demons place the sinners between two burning iron plates and press and rub them until their bodies become a bloody clay resembling a flaming red lotus.

### 15. *Stabbing Pain Hell*

Those who have promised to supply the sangha with necessary items and later, at the time of need, refuse to do so thereby causing great hardship, suffer here. The demons stab the sinners bodies with countless burning long iron needles. If a sinner opens his mouth to scream, the needles stab his tongue until it resembles an arrow quiver.

### 16. *Hell of Limitless Pain*

Destined for those who deceive others by conspiring to steal their fortune such as the guide who leads ships into the pirate's trap. The demons of this hell pull out the sinner's tongue and as soon as it grows back in again tender and soft, repeat the torment. They also use tongs to pluck out the sinner's eyes and they shave the flesh of the sinner's body with a sword just as a razor shaves the head. Worms also devour the sinner's intestines and countless other tortures are inflicted upon him.

### 17. *Hell Where the Blood and Bones Are Consumed*

Rulers or leaders who, after imposing one tax upon the populace later find it insufficient and demand a surcharge are punished here by being hung upside down from a burning tree. Crows with diamond beaks peck at their feet until the blood flows down and runs into their mouths. At the same time that they are forced to swallow their own blood, they are tormented by intense pains of hunger and thirst.

### 18. *Hell of Eleven Flames*

The ruler or respected man who arbitrates in a quarrel between two friends and unfairly discriminates against one because of a bribe, personal contact, or emotion and lies in his decision, falls into this hell. Here he is burnt by flames issuing forth from the ten directions and an internal burning flame of hunger and thirst. This internal flame is so intense that it spouts out of his mouth and consumes his tongue.

### F. *Tapana (Hell of Burning Heat)*

Major cause: False Views
Minor Hells:

## 1. Great Burning Hell

Those who believe that by sacrificing life they can be born into a deva heaven are tormented here by fires of intense heat 16 times greater than those found in any other hell. Besides the exterior and interior fires that burn the sinners, a third flame afflicting them is the burning regret within their minds.

## 2. Puṇḍarīka Hell

Individuals who mistakenly believe that they can obtain birth in a heaven by practicing starvation and teach such beliefs to others, are born in this hell. Here the sinners view a refreshing lotus forest in the distance with birds and cool water. The demons of the hell urge them to run to this peaceful haven and as they enter the pathway, they discover that it is filled with burning charcoal. Also there are firepits along the way that the sinners fall into. Despite many other torments such as being blinded by insects who eat out their eyes, the sinners finally reach the lotus forest, but in reality the forest is merely another inferno with lotus colored flames. The sinners deceived by their karma do not realize this and climb on top of the flaming lotuses seeking coolness and sit there until they are consumed by fire.

## 3. Circling Dragon Hell

Non-Buddhists who preach that men cannot obtain Nirvana by means of quieting desires, anger and ignorance fall into this hell inhabited by poisonous flaming headed dragons ranging in size from 1 krośa to 1 yojana. The entire hell is filled with these creatures and the sinners are pushed, squeezed and squashed by them until eventually they are pulverized. Some sinners are even born in the dragons' mouths where they are bitten by the poisonous fangs. Three fires torment the sinners of this hell: the fire of poison, the hell fires and the fire of hunger and thirst.

## 4. *Molten Copper and Mi-ni Fish Hell*

Those who preach that the world and all sentient beings are the creation of Maheśvara suffer in this place which is filled with flaming molten copper. An iron fish inhabits this boiling mass and chases the sinners until it catches them in its mouth. Then the sinners are forced to suffer doubly by having half their bodies burnt in the liquid and the other half bitten by the fish. There are also diamond beaked worms in the liquid that bite the sinners and when they attempt to open their mouths and scream out in agony, the molten copper pours within.

## 5. *Iron Caldron Hell*

Those who ritualistically sacrifice men or turtles, believing that when the sacrifice is born into a deva heaven they also will attain such a heaven suffer here. There are six different iron caldrons 10 yojana high containing various different tortures and the sinners are placed in each of them. These consist of:

    a. Pot where the sinners are cooked equally and unable to resist their torments

    b. Fiery molten copper pot

    c. Boiling salt water that slices the sinners' bodies as they bob up and down and cook like beans.

    d. Pot filled with sharp sword hair that slices bodies like thin razors.

    e. Extremely hot boiling water that splashes ½ yojana high.

    f. Pot filled with sharp-toothed evil snakes.

## 6. *Floating in a River of Blood Hell*

Those who have broken the Buddhist discipline and believe they can now obtain merit by practising extreme asceticism; thus go into a forest, hang themselves upside down and slash their faces and bodies with swords or knives in hope of obtaining heaven, are burnt here. The demons of the hell smashing the sinners with stones, halberds and swords create a river of rapidly flowing blood that sweeps the bodies along. A second river in this hell is filled with molten copper and fiery insects that bite the sinners and with the intense heat of their touch, explode the sinners' bodies into the river.

### 7. Bone Eating Insect Hell

Those who are hoping to be born in the Brahmā world and burn their bodies with dry cow dung suffer here. The sinners' bodies grow to fill the entire hell becoming 3 yojana wide and 5 yojana tall. After having become such a mountain of flesh, they are burnt by a fire 104 yojana high while the hell demons beat and pulverize them. In remembrance of all the insects they formerly destroyed, here the sinners are plagued in their mountains of flesh by worms and insects.

### 8. Hell Where Everyone Is Cooked

In this hell misguided individuals who, in hope of pleasing the fire deva and being born in a heaven, set fires in fields, mountains or forests, are tormented by the vision of loved ones being burnt in the hell fires. Having no method of saving them when these loved ones call upon the sinners for help, they are tormented by observing such suffering 16 times greater than being burnt in the hell fires.

### 9. Endless Submerging Hell

Those who in order to please the fire god, and obtain rebirth in a high heaven, place insects, snakes, deer or horses into the fire, suffer here. The demons of the hell force the sinners to climb steep flaming mountains where their hands, feet and bodies are burnt.

## 10. *Mahā-padma Hell*

Those who believe that by offering human sacrifices during rituals they can obtain rebirth wherever they choose end up in this hell where the lotus flowers have great diamond thorns that scrape and stab every part of the sinners' bodies.

## 11. *Dangerous Cliff Hell*

Individuals who practice water rituals in order to be born in a deva heaven are destined for this place. Within the hell there is a 100 yojana high cliff that even the birds cannot cross and one sinner of the hell assures the rest that if they can only climb this cliff, they will be able to escape from the hell. Because of his words, many sinners attempt to climb the cliff and as they begin to fall off of it, the rest return in fear only to find the demons awaiting them with iron hammers.

## 12. *Diamond Bone Hell*

Those who believe and teach that all existents come into being and disappear without any cause, just like a mirage, suffer here by having the demons peel off their flesh until only bones remain. After they have been reduced to skeletons their former enemies appear and grab their bones and beat them, smashing their skulls. Eventually the sinners' pieces are spread out all over the hell.

## 13. *Black Iron Rope and Pain of Release Hell*

Those who believe that all virtue and evil are predestined suffer here from being chained by iron ropes and then sliced with burning swords from head to toe.

## 14. *Crocodile Hell*

Men who teach either that nothing exists or that everything is eternal are tormented in this hell by having iron spears pierced through their bodies after which the crocodiles attack them and devour all their various parts.

### 15. Dark Fire Wind Hell

Those who teach that while the human body is impermanent, the four great elements are eternal and teach others such views are born into this hell where an evil wind blows them up into the air, spins them until they become invisible, and then smashes their bodies into dust.

### 16. Diamond Beak Hornet Hell

Destined for those who teach that the universe had an origin; they are tormented in this hell by the demons who pull all their hair roots out with thin pliers and stuff them into the sinners' mouths forcing them to eat them. There are also diamond beaked hornets that upon touching the sinners cause their blood to spurt out. The demons then force the sinners to drink this blood which has a bitter taste. The more the sinners eat and drink the more hungry they become until deceived by their minds they begin to chew on their own flesh.

### G. Pratapana (Hell of Great Burning Heat)

Major cause: Sexual defilement of religion
Minor Hells:

### 1. Hell Burning in All Directions

Those who rape virtuous laywomen following the Buddhist discipline are tormented in this hell of intense flame where there is not a single spot even the size of a needle without flame. When the sinners attempt to escape from this place, the demons capture them and tie them down with iron ropes and pull hooks through their chins in order to roll them over.

## 2. Fearful Hell of Large Roaring Bodies

The man who rapes a woman who has embarked upon the path to become a Buddhist nun suffers here by having his body grow to the size of one yojana while remaining extremely tender. The demons of the hell with delicate pliers pull out all of the sinner's hair and then proceed to peel off his flesh from head to toe. In this manner tremendous suffering is endured.

## 3. Burning Hell of String-like Worms

Destined for the man who deliberately engages in improper relations with a woman leading a virtuous life. Here the demons tie the sinners and place them on the burning hell floor studded with iron hooks. As they begin to cry out in agony, the demons then take a long bow-string shaped worm and insert it into their rectums. This worm with its sharp teeth, burning sensors and poisonous sting scorches its entrance into the body and proceeds to devour the entrails as it releases its painful poison. Gradually, it works its way upwards consuming whatever it touches until it arrives at the head. There, in order to make its escape, it cracks open a hole in the skull and slithers out. Escaping from this torment, the sinners encounter a nest of evil snakes, the creation of their own karma. These snakes coil around them, squeezing and striking their bodies.

## 4. Fire Rain Hell

Those who experience joy in defiling a woman on the pathway to becoming a Buddhist nun suffer here. The hell is filled with a great fire 500 yojana high and diamond-like triangular shaped sand. When the sinners enter into this sand, which is soft like water, they sink to the bottom and then bob up again. The sharp edges of the sand, eventually by rubbing their bodies a countless number of times, wear off the flesh. This grows back again so that the torture can be repeated a countless number of times.

### 5. *Place of Internal Boiling*

The man who deliberately defiles a virtuous laywoman believing that he has committed no sin and will receive no retribution suffers in this hell of five burning mountains that are filled with boiling flames. When the sinners observe these mountains they are deceived into believing that they see cool forests with flowers and lakes and rush to them. But as they reach this place they discover masses of burning flame and the sinners fall deep into the sides of the mountains just as an arrow pierces an ant hill.

### 6. *Shouting Hell*

Those who enter into improper practices that are basically sexual in nature with women who practice the Buddhist discipline a number of times, or have such a relationship with their own sisters or a member of their own sex, are tormented here. The winds of the hell blow the sinner's body up into the air and smash it into pieces no larger than grains of sand. When the body has once again returned to its normal shape, it is attacked by diamond-like evil rats that consume every organ.

### 7. *Hell of All Varieties of Suffering*

The monk possessing a mind of desire who tempts a virtuous woman following the discipline with liquor in order to have sexual relations with her and later rewards her with some form of gift is attacked in this hell by the demons who peel his skin from head to toe and then pour hot ashes over it.

### 8. *Place of Vetala*

The man who leads a virtuous woman to sin falls into this hell where burning iron sticks drop down like rain from the darkened skies and pierce the sinners' bodies. When they manage to escape from this suffering, they fall off a cliff and then arrive at a river filled with flame-fanged evil snakes.

## 9. *Hell of Total Darkness*

Those who send women to subdue virtuous Buddhists fall into this place where evil worms capable of breaking diamonds like bubbles, dwell. These worms attack them and crack open the marrow of their bones.

## 10. *Place of Painful Hair*

The woman who threatens a monk when he visits her home that if he refuses to have relations with her she will tell her husband that he raped her and if he will, she will provide him with food and drink and publicly announce that he is a holy man, is destined for this hell. Here the demons grab her and rub off her flesh with a sharp iron until only the bones remain. As soon as it is all gone, new flesh grows back and the torment is repeated. When she runs to escape, she sees the figure of the monk she had formerly tempted before her and filled with desire she embraces him but the moment that she touches him the vision bursts into flame.

## 11. *Hell called Yü-lü-man-tou-sou*

Those who take advantage of Buddhist nuns during the time when the land is in chaos suffer in this place where diamond sharp swords form a net covering every part of the hell. As the sinners move, their bodies are sliced and torn. Demons of the hell also shoot them with flaming arrows and as they run to escape, they visualize in the distance a large gate with a lantern burning in the middle of it. Rushing to arrive there in hopes of finding a door to escape, they find instead a huge poisonous snake that devours them.

## 12. *Hair Bird Hell*

The man who becomes intoxicated in order to fulfill his sexual desire for his elder or younger sister is cooked in this hell in a pot of molten copper until he melts. At other times the demons place him in the fire and heat it with bellows until the flames and sinners become indistinguishable, then they pluck him out and hammer him on an anvil.

### 13. *Place of Mourning and Pain*

Cultists who teach that a woman commits a crime and will be punished if she does not take every man that she desires, fall into this hell where they are pounded by the demons. In the distance they see a peaceful forest with cool lakes and hear the sound of bird singing there. Rushing to that haven they discover when they arrive that what they believed were trees was actually a large 1,000 headed dragon with burning eyes and the sound they thought was the singing of the birds was actually the screaming and lamenting of the sinners.

### 14. *Place of Great Tragedy*

The man, who upon hearing that a virtuous teacher or master has gone abroad, seduces his wife and then passes her off as his mother arrives in this hell. There is a burning iron floor studded with swords resembling sharpening blades. Here every part of the sinner's body is rubbed against the floor until the flesh and muscle disappear leaving merely bone.

### 15. *Hell of Absolute Darkness*

Destined for the man who has relations with his daughter-in-law. The demons of the hell cook the sinners on the hot ground until they form one solid piece and then pound them into a fine dough.

### 16. *Hell of Spinning Trees*

Reserved for those who have relations with the wife of a former benefactor who once saved their lives. Here the sinners are jammed together into a river of molten white pewter. They are so crowded that some float face upwards piled on top of the bodies of others and some float face downwards beneath the mass. Large fish inhabiting the river bite them and devour their flesh.

## H.  Avīci (Hell of No-interval)

Major cause: Five Sins.
Minor Hells:

### 1.  Bird Mouth Hell

Destined for those who deliberately murder an Arhat or receive joy by causing the body of the Buddha to bleed; who repeat such actions frequently and teach others. These sinners are born in this crow mouth hell where the suffering is one hundred times more painful than all the pains of the former seven major hells. The demons of the hell repeatedly rip off the mouths of the sinners, just as farmers tear off the mouth of the crow and as soon as it is torn off, a new mouth grows back in its place. The sinner also stumbles into a rapid flowing black lava river and as he opens his mouth to cry out, the lava flows within to sear his innards.

### 2.  Hell Where Everything Faces the Ground

Those who with a premeditated evil plan to force holy nuns or arhats into repeated sexual relations are laid face down on the burning iron ground by the demons of this hell and tossed back and forth. Although they attempt to scream in agony, they find they are unable to utter a sound. As they lie with bodies turned upward and faces twisted down, the demons of the hell hack at them with sharp axes until all their flesh is torn away. Then the demons proceed to wash their bones in molten lava and drop them on the ground. The sinners still live through all of these ordeals and suffer. At other times they are boiled in a pot of molten copper where they bubble up and down like beans.

### 3. Hell of Perpetual Suffering without any Shore of Escape

The type of man who is disturbed by a chaotic environment, possesses a mind of desire, and through association with evil friends, or because of drunkenness, engages in incest with his mother and later because of feelings of guilt seeks out an evil teacher to justify his action, then repeats his sin and encourages others to do likewise, suffers in this place of torment. The demons of the hell with flaming iron hooks catch the sexual organ of the sinner and pull it out, while at other times, stab it with spiked thorns. Another torment the sinner must endure is to be nailed to the ground with iron hooks that are driven through the nose, ears, and every part of the body.

### 4. Hell of Roaring Beasts

Those who abuse and criticize the man of Perfect Wisdom, a Pratyeka Buddha, Arhat, or the Dharma and Vinaya and preach contrary practices are condemned to this hell where they are chased by wild boar-like creatures possessing flaming iron mouths. As these animals catch the sinners they devour various parts of their bodies.

### 5. Hell of Being Devoured by Iron Beasts

Here those who with evil intention and premeditation burn temples belonging to the sangha, the image of the Buddha, bedding, clothing, grain or other properties of the sangha, or with evil intention set fire to the residence of the monks and feel no regret for their deeds; even counsel others to do the same, suffer. Every part of the body is burnt by a flame that becomes as tall as ten yojana. The sinners tormented by the fires of thirst and hunger seek to climb up the burning mountains of the hell and although they stretch their arms up as high as five yojana in an attempt to climb up and out of the hell, it is to no avail. As they shout and cry their mouths fill with flame. Even if they do manage to eventually escape from this place, they then find themselves in a place where chunks of iron as large as one krośa rain down upon them like a summer shower. Eventually, pulverized from head to toe, they die and again are restored to life. Still weak from all these ordeals they are chased by wild-boar-like creatures that devour parts of their bodies.

### 6. Hell of Black Bile

Destined for those who steal food and other objects from the Buddha. The sinners in this hell suffer from such extreme hunger and thirst that they devour their own bodies. Eventually, in an attempt to escape, they run to various places in the hell where they are then attacked by great black snakes that feed upon them.

### 7. Ocean of Bodies Hell

Those who steal from the Dharma suffer here by being rubbed to shreds between two great trees as they are moved by the wind. Also hard beaked birds attack the sinners and pluck out their eyes, tear out their hearts, and crack open their skulls in order to drink the juices of their brains.

### 8. Hell of Fearful Dreams

The place destined for those who steal food away from the sangha, and rejoice over their act as the monks suffer from hunger. Here a monstrous evil man carrying various types of torture instruments assails them. Rubbing the flesh off their bodies, he places them in an iron box and smashes them with a pounder until they become one congealed mass. After they return to life, he then proceeds to beat them with a stick. Even if the sinners manage to escape from this box, their karma leads them into a forest of iron trees where they are torn apart and crushed.

### 9. Hell Where Pain Is Received From the Ocean of Bodies

The man who wears Buddhist robes yet greedily takes from a

lay family the food, clothing and drugs they donate for the sick is tormented in this hell by the burning heat of a one yojana tall flaming tree. The sinner is born beneath the root of the tree hanging upside-down. Not only is he pressed by the weight of the tree and the heat, but he is also afflicted with 404 various diseases.

### 10. *Hell of Twin Mountains*

The man who snatches food away from a starving Pratyeka Buddha falls into this place where iron mountains one yojana high tumble down and crush him. Also various flames spurt out of his organs, molten copper is poured into his ears and he is afflicted with disease.

### 11. *Bird Hell*

Those who deliberately cut off the water supply to a land causing famine, death and desolation are born in this place where as a result of their reverted views, they imagine seeing a cool river and forest in the distance. Running to that place in hopes of escape from the fiery hell and seeking to quench their thirst, they discover that what they had believed to be refreshing water is actually burning ash. The demons of the hell then capture them and slice up their bodies with swords. Still suffering from thirst, they escape once more and visualize in the distance another river. In this river a bird as large as an elephant called Emba dwells and with its sharp beak it captures the sinners, then flies high into the air and drops them to be dashed to pieces on the ground.

### 12. *Hell of Sparks*

Destined for those who joyfully steal food from a hungry holy monk. In this hell there are two places of torment, one consists of a large pot where the sinners are cooked and boiled. The sparks of the flames of the pot resemble the stars in the sky and provides the name of the hell. In the second place the winds blow a countless number of swords through the air that slice the sinners' bodies.

## 13. *Hell of Rapid Pain*

The man with an evil mind, and reverted views who deliberately destroys the paintings or writings of the Buddha, causing the Dharma body to disappear, suffers here for his act of depriving some individuals of the opportunity to attain Enlightenment. In this hell the sinners have molten copper or hot coarse sand rubbed into their eyes. The fingers and hands that destroyed the Dharma are in turn cut off by sharp swords.

## 14. *Hell of Stench*

Those who deliberately destroy the sangha's agricultural fields, crops, orchards and burn their dwelling places suffer here from being herded by the demons of the hell who brandish bows and arrows and swords, into a burning net called the Needle Hole Net. The sinners become tangled with this net and its sharp edges pierce their bodies tearing away the flesh until only the bone remains.

## 15. *Hell of Iron Plates*

The malicious person who in the time of shortage and financial crisis promised to allow the monks to hold their retreat at his house and then later, when they arrive without having made any alternate plans, drives them away and causes them extreme suffering, is tormented here. The sinners are surrounded in the hell by eleven different flames and constantly suffer from hunger and thirst. Frequently the demons force them to drink molten copper juice or eat pieces of hot metal.

## 16. *Hell of Eleven Flames*

Reserved for those who practice evil and destroy the Buddha's image, stupa or residence of the sangha. Also for those who are not true Buddhist disciples but claim to be in order to criticize. Here they are bitten by poisonous snakes and burnt by extreme fires. The demons deliver long tirades to the sinners and then in rage torture them.

## FOOTNOTES TO INTRODUCTION

1. One example of a simple Japanese geta-maker who was able to intuitively comprehend the philosophical basis of Pure Land thought was Saichi Asahara (1850-1932). His simple writings were discovered by the late D. T. Suzuki and partially translated in his *Mysticism: Christian and Buddhist* (New York: Collier Books, 1962).

2. L. Austine Waddell, an early European critic of Buddhism, wrote in 1894 in *The Buddhism of Tibet or Lamaism* (2nd ed.; Cambridge: W. Heffer, 1959) p. 89 that the tortures of hell were "believed by the more philosophical Lamas to be morbid creations of the individual's own ideas, a sort of hellish nightmare." In 1932 Professor Shūgaku Yamabe published *Bukkyō ni okeru jigoku no shin kenkyū,* which is the only modern study available on the subject. Although Professor Yamabe's account is quite devotional, it represents an attempt to explore the deeper significance of hell as representing individual self-reflection.

## FOOTNOTES TO CHAPTER ONE

1. W. Norman Brown, "The Rigvedic Equivalent for Hell" in JAOS no. 61 (1941), pp. 76-80; A. A. Macdonell, *The Vedic Mythology* (Varanasi: Indological Bookhouse, 1963), p 169; H. D. Griswold, *The Religion of the Veda* (London: Oxford, 1923), p. 319; A. B. Keith, *The Religion and Philosophy of the Veda and Upanishads* (Cambridge: Harvard Univ., 1925), p. 409; Rudolph Roth, "Morality of the Veda" in JOAS no. 3 (1853), pp. 342-3.

2. Translated by Ralph T. H. Griffith, *Hymns of the Rigveda* (Benares: E. J. Lazarus, 1887), vol. 2, p. 98.

3. *Ibid.,* vol. 1, p. 296.

4. Brown, "The Rigvedic Equivalent for Hell," p. 78.

5. Translated by Paul Deussen, *The Philosophy of the Upanishads.* (Edinburgh: T. Clark, 1919), p. 321.

6. RV X. 14, 11-12. Griffith, *Hymns of the Rigveda,* Vol. 2, p. 399.

7. Translated by Griswold, *Religion of the Veda,* p. 380ff.

8. Sten Rodhe, *Deliver Us from Evil* (Copenhagen: Lund, 1946), p. 111.

9. See Maurice Bloomfield, *The Religion of the Veda* (London: Putnam, 1908), p. 194.

10. Keith, *Religion and Philosophy of the Veda and Upanishads,* p. 410.

11. Translated by Maurice Bloomfield, *Hymns of the Atharvaveda,* SBE (Oxford: Clarendon, 1897), p. 54.

12. XII. 9, 11.

13. VI. 2,2,27.

14. The entrance to the deva world is northeast. Sat. Brah. VI. 6.2,4 while the path to the world of the Fathers is southwest. Sat. Brah. XIII. 8, 15.

15. Sat Brah. XI. 6,2,5.

16. Translated by R. E. Hume, *The Thirteen Principal Upanisads* (London: Oxford Univ. 1958 ed.), p. 272.

17. *Ibid.,* p. 110.

18. *Ibid.,* p. 233.

19. The Buddhist chroniclers reported that four out of the six schools of thought contemporary to Buddhism denied this theory. They were led by Purana Kassapa, a nihilist, Makkhali Gosāla, who led the Ajivika school, Ajita Kesakambala, a materialist, and Pakudha Kaccayana, also a materialist. DN I 52-56.

20. S. Radhakrishnan, *Indian Philosophy,* Vol. I (London: Geo. Allen and Unwin, 1929 ed.), pp. 252-253.

21. *Ibid.,* p. 253.

## FOOTNOTES TO CHAPTER TWO

1. For a Buddhist summary of such practices see the *Brahmajāla Sutta* DN I, 9-13.

2. K. Mizuno, *Genshi bukkyō* (Kyoto: Heirakuji, 1961), pp. 66-7.

3. For a detailed explanation see Alicia Matsunaga, *The Buddhist Philosophy of Assimilation* (Tokyo: Sophia Univ. and Chas. E. Tuttle, 1969), pp. 5-16.

4. See AN IV 209ff.

5. See Issai Funahashi, *Genshi Bukkyō shisō no kenkyū* (Kyoto: Hōzōkan, 1962 ed.), p. 229.

6. Narada Thera trans. *The Dhammapada* (London: John Murray, 1959 ed.), p. 87. See also Pv 2.6.

7. SN I, 182.

8. MN II, 64.

9. See Funahashi, *Genshi Bukkyō shisō no kenkyū*, p. 237.

10. SN I, 33. Translated by Woodward, *Kindred Sayings*, Vol. I, p. 46.

11. *pañcasila*. AN III, 203.

12. SN I, 97.

13. "Santānaṇ punāti visodheti." Vimanavatthu Commentary, 19. Etymogically, *puñña* is most likely derived from *pu*, "to cleanse" or "to purify." See P.T.S.D. p. 464.

14. MN I, 90.

15. "Jatiya kho sati jara-maranam hoti, jati-paccaya jara-maranan ti." DN II, 31.

16. MN II, 32; III, 63; S II, 28; 95 etc.

17. SN IV, 207-208.

18. MN II, 32; III, 63; SN II, 28 and 95 etc.

19. SN II, 77.

20. Funahashi, *Genshi Bukkyō shisō no kenkyū*, p. 52.

21. This is the basis of the historical Buddha's famous Fourteen Silences regarding speculative philosophical questions on the nature of the world and life after death. MN I, 426 ff; as well as his subsequent preaching of the parable of the poisoned arrow. (*Ibid.*)

22. The historical Buddha made it very clear that the exterior world exists only so long as the individual is conscious of it (DN I, 215·23), meaning that it only has significance as it relates to individual experience and efforts towards salvation.

23. The historical Buddha himself spoke of receiving more merit as a result of virtuous actions. T. Vol. 2, p. 668.

24. Funahashi, *Genshi Bukkyō shisō no kenkyū*, p. 87.

25. Quoted by Buddhaghosa in the Khp Commentary I, 78.

26. Narada trans. *Dhammapada*, p. 15.

27. *Ibid.*, p. 77.

28. *Ibid.*, p. 47.

29. SN V, 447 AN II, 80.

30. See AN IV, 100 and the Dīgha Nikāya translation *Shih-chi-ching* (*Sekikyō*) T. Vol. 1, pp. 114-149, for a description of Mt. Sumeru and DN II, 107 or AN IV, 312 for the historical Buddha's explanation for earthquakes.

31. For a description of these in detail see W. Kirfel, *Die Kosmo-*

*graphie Der Inder* (Leipzig: Schroeder, 1920).

32. DN III, 234; AN IV, 459; SN V, 474-77; MN I, 73. In DN III, 264 the Asura (fighting spirits) are added to make the sixth existence although this practice was still apparently rare in Early Buddhism.

33. Snp. 126, also contained in AN V, 173; SN I, 150.

34. Snp. Commentary II, 477. The same commentary states that the names represent the sound of lamenting although some persons believed they were cold hells and the names were derived from the chattering of teeth.

35. AN I, 141; also MN III, 182 ff.

36. This addition is found in MN II, 185 ff.

37. Abhidharma schools are generally believed to have ranged in number between 18-26. See Mochizuki, *Bukkyō Daijiten,* Vol. 3, p. 2656-62.

38. T. Vol. 27, pp. 865-6. This explanation is followed by an alternate description in which five different varieties of earth form layers of 1,000 yojana each followed by the seven hells each 5,000 yojana square. The eighth hell remains the same, a 20,000 yojana square.

39. One yojana equals approximately nine miles.

40. T. Vol. 29, p. 61.

41. As an example, taking the Saṃghata or third hell, calculating the life-span according to these specifications it would consist of: $200 \times 360 \times 2,000 \times 360 \times 2,000 = 103,680,000,000,000,000$ years. In this manner as we descend further into the hells the number of years astronomically increases.

See Susumu Yamaguchi and Issai Funahashi, *Kusharon no genten kaimei* (Kyoto: Hōzōkan, 1957), p. 282.

42. SN II, 182.

43. SN II, 181.

# FOOTNOTES TO CHAPTER THREE

1. According to Reimon Yuuki, ed. *Bukkyō,* Vol. III (Tokyo: Daizō shuppansha, 1959, pp. 83-91, the key issues for the division mentioned in the existing vinaya texts refer to the dispute over 10 vinaya rules. This is the view held by the Southern tradition. The Northern tradition ascribes the division to the controversy over the Five Points concerning Mahādeva.

2. U. Wogihara and C. Tsuchida ed. *Saddharma Puṇḍarīka Sūtram* (Tokyo: Sankibō, 1958), p. 36.

3. One of the greatest errors of western writers in modern times

has been to place an undue emphasis upon this division and regard the two varieties as being radically different; i.e., Theodore Stcherbatsky, *The Conception of Buddhist Nirvana* (Leningrad: Academy of Science, 1927), p. 36.

4. The Sarvāstivāda school was the principal Abhidharma school attacked by the Mahāyānists. The works of this school have only been preserved in Chinese translation since the original Sanskrit is no longer extant. Ironically, this school played an influential role in the course of Mahāyāna development.

5. Modern Buddhist scholars even point out "Hīnayāna" views among the Mahāyānists such as clinging to the concepts of *Śūnyatā* or the Pure Land. See Susumu Yamaguchi, *Dynamic Buddha and Static Buddha* (Tokyo: Risōsha, 1958), pp. 55-57.

6. L. de La Vallée Poussin ed. *Mūlamadhyamaka kārikās de Nāggārjuna avec la Prasannadā de Candrakīrti* (St. Petersburg: Bibliotheca Buddhica, 1913), p. 11, and 592.

7. *Ibid.*, p. 349.

8. *Ibid.*, p. 214.

9. *Ibid.*, p. 209. Translated by Frederick J. Streng, *Emptiness, A Study in Religious Meaning* (Nashville: Abingdon Press, 1967), p. 195.

10. *Mūlamadhyamaka kārikās*, p. 341, trans. by Streng, *op cit.*, p. 204.

11. *Mūlamadhyamaka kārikās*, p. 57. Theo. Stcherbatsky in his glossary of *The Conception of Buddhist Nirvana* defines *prapañca* as "the expression of conceptually differentiated reality in words"; Streng. *Emptiness*, p. 251, translates is as "phenomenal extension"; K. V. Ramanan in *Nāgārjuna's Philosophy as Presented in the Mahā-prajñāparamitā Śāstra* (Rutland: Charles E. Tuttle, 1966), p. 399, uses "conceptual elaboration" and Richard Robinson in *Early Mādhyamika in India and China* (Madison: Univ. of Wisconsin, 1967), p. 341, defines it as "discursive fictions."

12. *Mahā-prajñāparamitā Śāstra* 192c trans. by Ramanan, *op. cit.*, p. 129.

13. *Mūlamadhyamaka kārikās* pp. 78-83; 182-183. See also Susumu Yamaguchi et al. *Bukkyōgaku josetsu* (Kyoto: Hōzōkan, 1961) pp. 129-130.

14. This may be the philosophical reason why Japanese Buddhist paintings depicting the coming of Amida (*Raigō*) are directed towards the dying. Since there is no actual heaven to attain after death at the philosophical level, we can only imagine that the dying person is in a unique position to attain Enlightenment.

15. See S. Yamaguchi, *Daijō to shite no Jōdo* (Tokyo: Risōsha, 1963) pp. 35-44; Akira Hirakawa, *Kōza Bukkyō* Vol. III (Tokyo:

Daizō shuppansha, 1959) p. 157.

16. *Mūlamadhyamaka kārikās,* p. 350. trans. by Streng, *Emptiness* p. 204. For a detailed explanation of these two aspects see Susumu Yamaguchi, *Kū no sekai* (Tokyo: Risōsha, 1940) p. 46.

17. *Mūlamadhyamaka kārikās* p. 531. Translated by Streng, *Emptiness,* p. 213.

18. *Mūlamadhyamaka kārikās* p. 592. Streng trans. p. 220.

19. *Mūlamadhyamaka kārikās de Nāgārjuna avec la Prasannapadā de Candrakīrti.* p. 50-51.

20. To present scriptural proof for his assertion, Candrakīrti quotes from the *Arya-upāliparipṛcchā* (Jap. *Shō uparimon bukkyō*) Nanjio 1109. The Sanskrit original of this text is no longer extant. The present Chinese translation is generally attributed to Guṇavarman in 431 A.D. although some sources state that it was made considerably earlier.

21. Walpola Rahula, "Asaṅga" in *Encyclopaedia of Buddhism,* Vol. II p. 139.

22. *Ibid.*

23. This view is set forth by Dignāga in his interpretation of the *Pratītya samutpāda* of consciousness in the *Ālambana parīkṣā.* T. vol. 31, p. 888.

24. *Ibid.*

25. Susumu Yamaguchi, *Seshin no Jōdoron* (Kyoto: Hōzōkan, 1963) p. 160.

26. From the *Kanjinkakumushō,* a Japanese interpretation of Vijñānavāda thought written by Ryōhen in 1244 and quoted in Mochizuki, *Bukkyō daijiten* Vol. 2 p. 1582.

27. *Ibid.*

28. *Myōkōnin Asahara Saichishū* (Tokyo: Shunjūsha, 1967). The concept of the term *myōkōnin* (wondrously good man) is related to the notion of the lotus (*myōkōke,* wondrously good flower) arising out of the muddy waters with pure untouched petals.

29. Translated from *Myōkōnin Asahara Saichishū* p. 18 notebook 2 poem 12.

30. *Ibid.* p. 29, notebook 3 poem 8. In this instance the 'eyes' refer to the attitude of the viewer.

31. *Ibid.* p. 79, notebook 6 poem 40. The Namu Amida Butsu is an invocation of the name of the mythological Buddha Amida (Skt. Amitābha) used by the so-called Pure Land sects. Saichi understood the *namu* (lit. 'I take refuge') as representing the subjectivity and Amida as symbolic of ultimate reality with the invocation uniting the two into oneness. Elsewhere he described this union more poetically in the following manner:

. . . Let's celebrate,
Drink the Amida sake,
Eat the *namu* fish,
Its a merry Namu Amida Butsu.

p. 118 notebook 9 conclusion of poem 19.

32. *Ibid.* p. 18, notebook 14 poem 40.
33. *Ibid.* p. 187 notebook 14 poem 112.

## FOOTNOTES TO CHAPTER FOUR

1. For a discussion of the date of composition and author, see Prof. Shūgaku Yamabe's introduction to the Japanese edition in *Kokuyaku Issaikyō* (Tokyo, 1933) Vol. 8, pp. 1-7.
2. p. 27.
3. p. 28.
4. This metaphor first appeared in Early Buddhism. SN II, 94.
5. p. 29.
6. *Shibunritsu* (Dharmagupta vinaya) 42 T. Vol. 22, p. 866.
7. *Tannishō* contained in Daiei Kaneko ed. *Shinshūseiten* (Kyoto: Hōzōkan, 1960) p. 786.
8. Mizumaro Ishida ed. *Ōjōyōshū* (Tokyo: Heibonsha, 1965) p. 13. This view is drawn from the *Yugaron* (Yogācāra-bhūmi) and *Chidoron* (Mahāprajñāpāramitāśāstra).
9. Ishida, *Ōjōyōshū* p. 13, drawn from the *Kambutsu sammaikyō* (Buddhadhyāna-samādhisagara-sūtra).
10. This view is mainly derived from Prof. Shūgaku Yamabe's interpretation of this hell in *Bukkyō ni okeru jigoku no shin kenkyū* (Tokyo: Shunjūsha, 1932) pp. 76-79.
11. p. 32.
12. p. 66.
13. Vin. I, 34; S. IV, 20.
14. p. 44.
15. *Adbhutadharmaparyāya* (Jap. *Mizōu-innen-gyō*) T. vol. 17, p. 585.
16. See Prof. Issai Funahashi, Bukkyō-nyūmon (Kyoto: Hōzōkan, 1958, p. 82.
17. p. 44.
18. The subdivisions are also increased in number and this is the only major hell having eighteen subdivisions, each of which are treated in considerable detail.
19. AN V, 174. The same quotation appears in this sutra, p. 46.
20. See the *Sāmañña-phala sutta* DN I, 47-86.
21. DN II, 9.

22. p. 67.
23. This section is primarily aimed at the laity.
24. p. 76.
25. *Milinda pañha,* 310; Shibunritsu T. Vol. 22, p. 588.
26. *Bommōkyō* T. Vol. 24, p. 1006.
27. Narada Thera, trans. *The Dhammapada,* p. 43.
28. p. 182.
29. p. 234.

# BIBLIOGRAPHY

The majority of primary sources are taken from the following series:

*Abbreviations*

T. Taishō shinshū daizōkyō 55 vol. (1922-33)
*Pāli Text Society Series (London)*
AN  Aṅguttara Nikāya 5 vol. (1885-1900)
DN  Dīgha Nikāya 3 vol. (1960, 1966, 1967 reprints)
MN  Majjhima Nikāya 3 vol. (1887-1902)
SN  Saṃyutta Nikāya 5 vol. (1887-1902)
Snp  Sutta Nipāta (1913)

Bloomfield, Morris. *Hymns of the Atharvaveda,* Oxford, 1897.
———— *The Religions of the Veda,* London, 1908.
Brown, W. Norman. "The Rigvedic Equivalent for Hell" in *Journal of the American Oriental Society* no. 61 (1941) pp. 76-80.
Deussen, Paul. *The Philosophy of the Upanishads.* Edinburgh, 1919.
Dutt, N. *Early History of the Spread of Buddhism and Buddhist Schools,* London, 1925.
Fujita, Kōtatsu. *Genshi jōdoshisō no kenkyū.* Tokyo, 1970.

Fukaura, Seibun. "Alaya-vijñāna" in *Encyclopaedia of Buddhism* Vol. I pp. 382-388.

Funahashi, Issai. "Genshi Bukkyō ni okeru shukkedō to zaikedō" in *Indogaku Bukkyōgaku kenkyū*, Vol. II no. 1 (1954), pp. 34-43.

———— *Genshi Bukkyō shisō no kenkyū*, Kyoto, 1962 ed.

———— *Gō no kenkyū*, Kyoto, 1961.

Govinda, Anagarika. *Foundations of Tibetan Mysticism*, London, 1962 ed.

———— *The Psychological Attitude of Early Buddhist Philosophy* London, 1961.

Griffith, Ralph T. H. *Hymns of the Rigveda* 2 vol. Benares, 1887.

Griswold, H. D. *The Religion of the Rig Veda*, London, 1923.

Hirakawa, Akira. *Genshi Bukkyō no kenkyū*. Tokyo, 1964.

Hoshino, Genpō. *Jōdo*, Kyoto, 1965.

Ishida, Mizumaro. *Jōdokyō no tenkai*, Tokyo, 1967.

———— ed. *Ōjōyōshū*. Tokyo, 1964.

Iwamoto, Hiroshi. *Gokuraku to jigoku*, Tokyo, 1965.

Kaneko, Daiei. *Jōdosanbukyō to jōdoron no gaiyō*. Kyoto, 1963.

Keith, A. B. *The Religion and Philosophy of the Veda and Upanishads*. Harvard, 1925.

Kubose, Gyōmay. *Everyday Suchness*. Chicago, 1967.

Law, Bimala Charan. *Heaven and Hell in Buddhist Perspective*, Calcutta, 1925.

Macdonnell, A. A. *The Vedic Mythology*. Varanasi, 1963.

Matsunaga, Alicia. *The Buddhist Philosophy of Assimilation*. Tokyo, 1969.

Miyamoto, Shōson. ed. *Bukkyō no kompon shinri*, Tokyo, 1957.

———— *Chūdōshiso oyobi sono hattatsu*, Kyoto, 1944.

———— "The Middle Way from the Standpoint of the Dharma" in *Indogaku Bukkyōgaku kenkyū* Vol. 17 no. 2 (1969) pp. 963-932.

Mizuno, K. *Genshi Bukkyō*. Kyoto, 1961.

Murti, T. R. V. *The Central Philosophy of Buddhism*. London, 1960.

Nakamura, Hajime. *Indoshisōshi*, Tokyo, 1956.

———— *Ways of Thinking of Eastern Peoples*. Honolulu, 1964.

Narada Thera trans. *The Dhammapada.* London, 1954 ed.

Poussin, L. de la Vallée, ed. *Mūlamadhyamaka kārikās de Nāgārjuna avec le Prasannadā de Candrakīrti.* St. Petersburg, 1913.

Ramanan, K. V. *Nāgārjuna's Philosophy as Presented in the Mahā-Prajñāparamitā śāstra,* Rutland, 1966.

Robinson, Richard. *Early Mādhyamika in India and China.* Madison, 1967.

Rhode, Sten. *Deliver Us From Evil.* Studies on the Vedic Ideas of Salvation. Copenhagen, 1946.

Roth, Rudolph. "Morality of the Veda" trans. by Wm. . Whitney in *Journal of the American Oriental Society* 3 (1853) pp. 329-347.

Sawada, Mizuho. *Jigokuhen,* Kyoto, 1968.

Stcherbatsky, Theodore. *The Conception of Buddhist Nirvana.* Leningrad, 1927.

Streng, Frederick. *Emptiness, A Study in Religious Meaning* Nashville, 1967.

Suzuki, Daisetsu. *Jōdokei shisōron,* Kyoto, 1966.

———*Myōkōnin Asahara Saichishū,* Tokyo, 1967.

Tucci Giuseppe, *The Theory and Practice of the Mandala,* New York, 1970 ed.

Watanabe, Shōkō. *Shigo no sekai.* Tokyo, 1960.

Wogihara, U. and C. Tsuchida ed. *Saddharma Puṇḍarīka sūtram,* Tokyo, 1958.

Yamaguchi, Kōen, *Tendai jōdokyōshi,* Kyoto, 1968.

Yamaguchi, Susumu, *Chūron shaku* 2 Vol. Tokyo, 1947.

———*Daijō to shite no jōdo,* Tokyo, 1960.

——— "Development of Mahayana Buddhist Beliefs" in Kenneth Morgan ed. *The Path of the Buddha,* New York, 1956.

———*Seshin no jōdoron,* Kyoto, 1963.

——— and Nozawa. *Seshin Yuishiki no genten kaimei,* Kyoto, 1953.

Yamabe, Shūgaku. *Jigoku no shin kenkyū,* Tokyo, 1932.

# INDEX

## A

Abhidharma Buddhism 38, 39, 43-
  46, 48, 49, 75, 141
Abhidharmakośa 45
abortion 83
action wisdom 65, 66
Ālaya vijñāna 61, 62, 63, 65, 66
Amida (Amitābha) 70, 141, 142
anātman (anattā) 28, 56, 68, 77
Aṅguttara Nikāya 41
Animal Realm 40, 77
Arhat (Arahant) 39, 87, 100, 131-
  132
Arūpa loka (World of non-form)
  39
Asahara, Saichi 69-70, 137
Asaṅga 60
Atharva Veda 15-16
Avīci (Hell of no-interval) 41, 44,
  45, 80, 99-103, 131-136
avidyā (avijjā) 29, 35, 36, 51

## B

birth and death 19, 28-29, 32, 33,
  36-38, 39, 68, 76
Black Rope Hell (Kāla sūtra) 44,
  80, 85-86, 109-111

Bone-eating Insect Hell 96-97, 124
Brahmā 19, 96, 124
Brahmacarya 25-26
Burning Hell of String-like Worms
  97-98, 127
Burning Sermon 90

## C

Candrakīrti 61, 142
Chandala Hell 86, 110
consciousness 29-30, 36, 39, 43,
  50, 61-69
Crowded Hell (Saṃghāta) 44, 80,
  87-90, 111-113

## D

dāna 26-27, 77, 94, 98
dāna kathā 24
Dark fire-wind hell 95, 126
death (see also birth and death) vii,
  14, 20, 27, 28, 32-34, 41, 55, 72
Dependent characteristic (paratantra lakṣaṇa) 65, 66-68
deva 17, 19, 22, 23, 24, 38, 40, 77,
  94-95, 100, 103-105, 125
Dhammapada 25, 38, 102
Dhammapāla 27

Dharma (Dhamma) 57, 58, 76, 78-79, 89, 98, 101, 102, 132, 133, 135
Diamond-beak Hornet Hell 95, 125
Diamond Bone Hell 96, 125
Discriminative Fully Assumed Characteristic (parikalpita lakṣaṇa) 63, 65, 66-68
dogs of Yama 14, 15
drugs 58, 86, 92

## E

Early Buddhism 21-43, 50, 61, 73, 83-84, 100
ecology 52
Emptiness (see 'śūnyatā) 54-60, 77
Enlightenment (see Nirvana) viii, 24, 26, 34-35, 38, 48, 54, 55, 56, 57, 58, 59, 61, 64, 66, 67, 70, 71, 72, 73, 78, 84, 90, 94, 96, 99, 101, 102, 105-106, 141
equality wisdom 65, 66

## F

false views (see Tapana Hell) 80, 94-97, 121-126
fire and firewood analogy 50-51
fire-jar Hell 89-90, 113
Five Existences 39-40, 75, 76-78
five sense consciousnesses 62-63, 65, 66
Five sins (Five forms of Opposition) 80, 99-102, 131-136
Fully Completed characteristic (parinispanna lakṣaṇa) 65, 67, 68

## G

Genshin 76, 85
Great Screaming Hell (Mahāraurava) 44, 80, 92-94, 117-121

## H

Hell of Burning Heat (Tapana) 44, 80, 94-97, 121-126
Hell of Complete Darkness 91, 115
Hell of Great Burning Heat (Pratapana) 44, 80, 97-99, 126-131
Hell of No-interval (Avīci) 44, 80, 99-103, 131-136
Hell of Rapid Pain 101, 135
Hell of Repetition (Saṃjīva) 44, 80, 81-85, 107-109
Hell of Unbearable Pain 93, 117-118
Hell Where Everyone is Cooked 95, 124
Hīnayāna ix, 47-48, 75, 91, 141
historical Buddha viii, 22, 23, 25, 28, 36, 38, 47, 49, 71, 90, 91, 92, 94, 96, 102, 139
Human realms 40
hungry ghosts (see preta)

## I

ignorance (see also avidyā) 29, 33, 35, 36, 51-53, 57-58, 62, 63, 64, 68, 70, 72, 88-89
Interdependent Origination (also see Pratītya samutpāda) 28-38, 48-49, 79, 84, 101-102, 106
intoxicants 80, 90-92, 114-117
iṣṭāpūrta 15

## J

Jambudvīpa (Jambudīpa) 39, 43-44
Jōdo Shinshū sect 69, 84, 91

## K

Kāla sūtra (Black-rope Hell) 44, 45, 80, 85-86, 109-111
kalpa 45
Kāma loka (see Five Existences) 39-40

karma (kamma) 15, 18-20, 21-22,
  24-27, 30, 35-38, 40, 42, 52, 78-
  79, 81, 82, 85, 86, 93, 94, 95,
  104
killing 27, 29, 80, 81-85, 86, 100-
  102, 107-109

L

love, 88-89, 106
lying 27, 29, 80, 92-94, 117-121

M

Mādhyamika ix, 46, 50-60, 61, 70,
  75
Mahāraurava (Great Screaming
  Hell) 44, 45, 80, 92-94, 117-121
Mahāvibhāṣa 43
Mahāyāna ix, 47-73, 75, 91, 93
Majjhima nikāya 26
meat eating 83-84
mental functions 62, 65, 66

N

Nāgārjuna 49-60, 64, 93
Nirvana (nirvāṇa) 25, 26, 35, 38,
  39, 61, 65, 69, 71, 98, 103, 113,
  122 (also see Enlightenment)
No-interval Hell (Avīci) 41, 45, 80,
  99-103, 131-136
notion of ego 62, 65, 66

O

observation wisdom 65, 66
Ōjōyōshū 76, 85

P

Parable of Arrow 33-34
Place of Darkness 81-82, 108
Place of Excrement 42, 81, 103
Place of Painful Hair 98, 129
prapañca 53, 58, 93, 141

Pratapana (Hell of Great Burning
  Heat) 44, 45, 80, 97-99, 126-
  131
pratītya samutpāda (paṭicca-samuppāda) 28-35, 38, 48-49, 51, 53,
  54, 57, 79, 101
Preta realm (petti visaya) 40, 77
Puṇḍarīka Hell 41, 94-95, 122
puñña 24-27, 98, 139
Pure Land (see Realm of Purification) 69-72, 76, 137, 142

R

Raurava (Screaming Hell) 44, 45,
  80, 90-92, 114-117
Realm of Pollution 59, 63-70
Realm of Purification 59, 63-72, 79,
  84
Ṛg Veda 13-15

S

Saddharma puṇḍarīka sūtra 48
Saddharma smṛti upasthāna sūtra ix,
  75-105, 107-136
sagga kathā 24
Samghāta (Crowded Hell) 44, 45,
  80, 87-90, 111-113
Samjīva (Hell of Repetition) 44, 45,
  80, 81-85, 107-109
samsāra 19, 38, 59, 69, 71
Samyutta Nikāya 25, 33
sankhāra 29-30, 35, 36
Screaming Hell (Raurava) 44, 80
  90-92, 114-117
sexual indulgence 27, 29, 80, 87-90,
  111-113
Shinran 84, 91
sīla kathā 24
Sisiphus 88
stealing 27, 29, 80, 85-87, 88, 109-
  111
śūnyatā 46, 48, 49, 50, 53, 57, 59,

61, 64, 67-68
'śūnyatā artha 55, 57-58, 59
'śūnyatāyām prayojanam 55, 56-57, 59

## T

Tapana (Hell of Burning Heat) 44, 45, 80, 94-97, 121-126
Theravāda 83-84, 91
Three Worlds 38, 39
Trayastrimśa 45
Tuṣita 45

## U

upāya 24, 40, 41, 46, 57-58, 102,

103, 105
upside-downness (viparyāsa) 60, 79-80, 99, 100, 112

## V

Vasubandhu 60
vijñāna (viññāṇa) 30, 35, 36, 50-51, 60-69
Vijñānavāda ix, 60-72, 75

## Y

Yama 14, 16, 19-20, 41
Yama heaven 45
Yogācāra (see Vijñānavāda)